JUNK
CHIC

*One man's junk is
another man's treasure.*
—Author Unknown

JUNK CHIC

KATHRYN ELLIOTT

Sterling Publishing Co., Inc. New York

A Sterling / Chapelle Book

ACKNOWLEDGMENTS

My deepest thanks to Jo Packham
and her incredible staff at Chapelle
for their vision of this book
and their belief in me.

A big hug to editor, Cathy Sexton,
who deserves a medal
for deciphering the "chaos" and
turning it into something wonderful.

My love and my heart
to Mama and her "make-it" cupboard
and to Daddy for being a real "daddy."

Library of Congress Cataloging-in-Publication Data

Elliott, Kathryn.
    Junk chic / Kathryn Elliott.
        p.   cm.
    "A Sterling/Chapelle book."
    Includes index.
    ISBN 0-8069-2514-0
    1. House furnishings. 2. Interior decoration.
3. Painting. I. Title.

    TX311.E45 2001   00-053194
    645–dc21   CIP

10 9 8 7 6 5 4 3 2 1

First paperback edition published in 2002 by
Sterling Publishing Company, Inc.
387 Park Avenue South, New York, N.Y. 10016
© 2001 by Kathryn Elliott
Distributed in Canada by Sterling Publishing
C/o Canadian Manda Group, One Atlantic Avenue, Suite 105
Toronto, Ontario, Canada M6K 3E7
Distributed in Great Britain and Europe by Cassell PLC
Wellington House, 125 Strand, London WC2R 0BB, England
Distributed in Australia by Capricorn Link (Australia) Pty. Ltd.
P.O. Box 704, Windsor, NSW 2756 Australia

Printed and Bound in China
All Rights Reserved

Sterling ISBN 0-8069-2514-0 Hardcover
                0-8069-7679-9 Paperback

Chapelle:

Jo Packham, Owner

Cathy Sexton, Editor

Staff: Areta Bingham, Kass Burchett, Marilyn Goff, Holly Hollingsworth, Susan Jorgensen, Kimberly Maw, Barbara Milburn, Linda Orton, Karmen Quinney, Leslie Ridenour, Cindy Stoeckl, Gina Swapp, Kim Taylor, Sara Toliver, Kristi Torsak

Photography: Kevin Dilley for Hazen Imaging, Inc., and Scot Zimmerman

If you have any questions or comments or would like information on specialty products featured in this book, please contact:

Chapelle, Ltd., Inc.
P.O. Box 9252, Ogden, UT 84409
(801) 621-2777 • (801) 621-2788 Fax
e-mail: chapelle@chapelleltd.com
website: www.chapelleltd.com

ABOUT THE AUTHOR

Me on a good day.

Me the other 364 days a year—"project days."

Kathryn Elliott has worked as a design consultant for over 15 years. She is an accomplished artist and has sold her works successfully through galleries in Palm Springs and Malibu, California. She works as a free-lance decorative paint artist and muralist, as well an instructor on faux and decorative paint techniques.

Clients of her hand-painted furniture pieces often have her do "make-overs" on their own existing furnishings. She is a self-proclaimed "junkophile" and is addicted to "junking."

Kathryn has been married for 22 years to the love of her life and together they have six children who keep it all "real." They currently reside in West Linn, Oregon.

This book is dedicated to my precious family and their tireless support of my vision—to make my world a beautiful place.

CONTENTS

CREATING SOMETHING FROM NOTHING

The entire process of decorating is nothing more than making changes to existing spaces. The desired result is a more visually appealing space that flows in a pattern more conducive to one's life-style. In this book you will discover new ways to decorate by altering existing finishes on the surfaces and furnishings of your home.

Through beautiful color photographs, I will take you room by room, project by project, through my own home, revealing fabulous rejuvenated junk-store style.

This is what the house looked like when we bought it. It had been rented for three years and the owners were anxious to sell. The terms and the view are what sold us—the rest is a testament to patience and vision.

Each project—from faux rocks made from brown paper grocery bags to a thrift-store coffee table that found new life as a gourmet kitchen pot rack—is made simple through detailed materials lists and step-by-step instructions.

Most of my house is furnished with second-hand items that have been transformed. I think of the walls as blank canvas to be painted on—oftentimes transporting the room to a new level through the paint treatment used.

When I was a little girl, my mom would save scraps of fabric, interesting-shaped boxes, snippits of trim, and general craft items in a designated "make-it" cupboard. When I was bored, that's where I went to entertain myself.

My inspiration still comes from a "make-it" cupboard—the one inside my head. When I come across something that I think is unattractive, my right brain kicks into overdrive trying to make it into something wonderful!

A very wise man once said, "Even a barn door looks better painted." Case in point—me! My concept of decorating goes hand-in-hand with this principle. A lot can be done with very little by using what you have on hand or what you find on a second-hand basis.

After nine years of doing and redoing, we had turned the "lunch box" house into a charmer. At the time this photo was taken we were no longer planting new flowers, they were filling in beautifully every year.

Most of us live in homes that need some updating, either structurally or cosmetically. This book will give you ideas on how to breathe new life into tired interiors and furnishings with projects that take little time and money. I will not only show you how to create these projects, but will give you inspiring, fresh ideas on how you can incorporate them into your own home to enhance and beautify your surroundings.

You will discover that a wide array of "treasures" are awaiting you at yard sales, thrift stores, and flea markets. With techniques presented in this publication, you will find inspiration and instruction on how-to transform these ugly ducklings into swans.

So, if you have always wanted a beautiful home on a shoestring budget, then *Junk Chic* is a book you cannot do without.

Let's face it, things don't need to be expensive to be beautiful!

Even with the kitchen as dark, dreary, and outdated as it was, our son Casey (10) enjoyed an evening cuddle with our cat Ozzie. The linoleum floor had been laid on top of two other layers of old flooring. We had to rent a special machine to pull it up. We did all the work—from removing the old cupboards to assembling the new ones.

BEFORE YOU BEGIN

Whenever you begin a painting project, make certain to cover any exposed floors or table surfaces with adequately sized drop cloths. This simple task will make the project more enjoyable and will save hours of clean-up and possible repair. In addition, it is important to work in a well-ventilated area, as many paint products have toxic fumes.

Read manufacturers' directions and recommendations when using any product for the first time. The labeling will be your best source of important information pertaining to that product.

When selecting a sealer, choose one that is compatible with the paint you are using. If you are using water-based paint, use a water-based sealer. If you are using oil-based paint, use an oil-based sealer. Mixing the two could cause the sealer to act as a stripping agent and the paint could begin to bubble.

In high-traffic areas you will want to use latex paint instead of acrylic craft paint. Latex paint will extend the life of your projects and makes cleaning easier.

It is my policy to always use what is around the house before going out and buying new supplies and materials. Check your existing resources—this also goes for project pieces. Look around your house or garage for furniture that can be recycled into a new life in a different space of your home. You will surprise yourself at what you already have to work with.

Never panic! Remember . . . it's just paint. If you make a mistake, cover it and start over.

Lastly, be especially nice to your family. They will have to put up with the interruption in their lives and with your passion for great-looking junk!

WELCOME TO OUR HOME

When we first drove up to the house with our realtor, my husband Rob refused to get out of the car to go inside. He thought the house looked like a giant lunch pail! But after a little coaxing, we convinced him that he needed to at least "humor" me. Together we agreed that the view was so spectacular that we could overlook all of the other flaws and decided to make the leap. I immediately went to work, relying on the skills I had acquired through a lifetime of creating something from nothing.

The process of turning this house on Emerald Hills into a "gem" of a home has been a labor of love and an adventure in stretching the limits of my own creativity, invention, and vision.

So, come on in! Leave your doubts and inhibitions at the front door and discover the exciting world of "Junk Chic."

KITCHEN & FAMILY ROOM

WINDOW CORNICE & CURTAIN

My husband Rob is a genius when it comes to figuring out how to execute all of my crazy ideas. This is yet another example of his prowess!

The window area above our kitchen sink was architecturally flat. In addition, it needed softening—something I believed curtains could provide. However, I did not want a traditional window treatment here. This area needed a tie-in to the computer center Rob had recently finished at the opposite end of the kitchen. Something in a wood finish was needed to warm up this space in contrast to the high-gloss white cupboards.

Rob designed the window cornice and built it from pine. I attached the plaster lion medallion with construction adhesive, caulked the edges, and painted it in the same color and technique as the other side of the kitchen.

I used a chain to simulate distressed wood on the face of the cornice, then accentuated the dents with a brown craft paint wash.

For the window treatment, I chose a tapestry fabric with the rich tones and European feel I wanted. The fabric was simply folded in half, lengthwise, and nailed to the inside of the cornice with small finishing nails. It also could have been attached with a staple gun. The pleats were created by folding the fabric in two places toward the center of the pleat and secured with nails. No sewing was required.

The window cornice with curtains attached was mounted to the wall with three "L" brackets placed under the top piece of the cornice.

FAUX TUMBLED TILE

Most wallpaper stores offer at least three different patterns of embossed wallpaper. The styles that are already shaped like tile work best for this application.

MATERIALS

- Embossed wallpaper
- Paintable acrylic latex caulk
- Nylon paintbrush: 6" flat
- Craft paints: dark sand, light taupe, white
- Synthetic sponges
- Satin acrylic sealer

WHAT TO DO

- Step 1: Measure, cut, and install the wallpaper in the desired area(s). Let dry.

- Step 2: Caulk all the edges next to walls, counters, and cupboards. Let dry.

- Step 3: Using a paintbrush, apply a base coat of dark sand paint onto the wallpaper. Let dry.

- Step 4: Using a damp sponge, lightly rub light taupe paint onto the embossed areas of the wallpaper over the coat of dark sand. Let dry.

- Step 5: Using a dry sponge, randomly sponge white paint onto the embossed areas of the wallpaper over the coat of light taupe to give a whitewashed look. Let dry.

- Step 6: Using a damp sponge, slightly rub the coats of paint in a random pattern to remove some of the paint.

- Step 7: Using the paintbrush, seal the wallpaper. Let dry.

- Step 8: Additional coats of sealer may be applied. Let dry between each coat.

DECORATING TIPS

- Any color can be used.

- These tiles work well in a bathroom, but they must be sealed with a high-gloss sealer to protect them from the moisture.

- Embossed wallpaper can be applied to dresser drawer fronts and painted using this technique.

COFFEE TABLE POT RACK

This pot rack is not just great looking—it is also functional! This $10 thrift-store coffee table was transformed into a piece of kitchen furniture by adding some copper pipe, metal hooks, and curtain rod finials.

MATERIALS

- Coffee table
- Wood screws
- Hacksaw
- Copper pipe
- "S" hooks to fit onto the copper pipe
- Copper brackets
- 4 Curtain rod finials

WHAT TO DO

- Step 1: Decide where you are going to hang the "pot rack." If studs are available in the ceiling, use wood screws to hang the table.

If studs are not available, use molly bolts to hang the table. When using molly bolts, predrill pilot holes in the table and in the ceiling.

- Step 2: Hoist the table into mounting position and secure it onto the ceiling.

- Step 3: Using a hacksaw, cut the copper pipe. To calculate the lengths of copper pipe needed, determine where you want the ends to be—only two sides can extend past the table length. Cut two pieces the same length as the table and two pieces the same length plus 2" as the table width.

- Step 4: Thread the "S" hooks onto all four lengths of copper pipe.

You will need enough of these hooks to hold the pots and pans you plan to hang.

- Step 5: Anchor the copper brackets into place around the copper pipe on all four sides of the table with wood screws. If the table is rectangular, use one additional copper bracket at the center of each long side.

- Step 6: Place a curtain rod finial into each open end of copper pipe.

This functional piece of kitchen furniture makes it unnecessary to ever put the pots and pans away in the cupboard again. Keep in mind that when you hang your pots and pans, you will want to distribute the weight as evenly as possible.

IRON URNS

These two urns received a makeover to fit in with our kitchen colors and decor. They had originally been green and were on display in the living room bookcase.

I lightly sanded them and painted them with flat black spray paint, then sponged them with dark brown craft paint. I used the same color of brown craft paint that I used on the Tarnished Brass Chandelier on page 26 that hangs above them.

These urns are frequently filled with fruits or flowers—depending on the season! Because of their dark color, they show-off just about anything we display in them.

DECORATING TIPS

• Try putting similar-sized urns on old books to give them added height and importance.

• Adding a large candle to the center of each urn will create incredible ambiance.

• To raise the level of your arrangements, layer the bottoms of the urns with newspaper, then cover the newspaper with dried moss.

TARNISHED BRASS CHANDELIER

The weathered finish on this dated brass chandelier was achieved with sandpaper, craft paint, and acrylic sealer. The lamp shades were painted black to add intimacy to the dining area.

MATERIALS

- Brass chandelier
- Lamp shades
- 100-grit sandpaper
- Synthetic sponge
- Craft paint: brown
- Foam brush: 2" flat
- Satin acrylic sealer
- Spray paint: black

WHAT TO DO

- Step 1: Sand the chandelier and wipe clean.
- Step 2: Using a damp sponge, randomly sponge brown craft paint onto the chandelier.
- Step 3: Using the damp sponge, press brown craft paint onto the chandelier and let it "drizzle" down the surface. Let dry.
- Step 4: Repeat the drizzling process until the desired effect is achieved. Let dry.
- Step 5: Using a foam brush, seal the chandelier. Let dry.
- Step 6: Paint the lamp shades with black spray paint. Let dry.
- Step 7: Install the chandelier.

DECORATING TIPS

- Any metallic surface can be "tarnished" using this method, including candlesticks, table lamps, or brass planters.
- If the surface you are using is not metallic, you can paint the surface with any metallic-toned spray paint and continue the process using the same method.
- Bargain lamp shades may be painted in matching metallic tones or covered with fabric to tie in with your decor.

FAUX WASHED PLASTER

The walls in the kitchen had been a dark green. When the living room was elderberry burgundy, the green was suitable; but after I weathered the living room walls, the two spaces didn't flow.

This is a great example of using "what you have on hand." I used the leftover paint from the living room and created a different, but harmonious feel in the kitchen and adjoining computer area.

MATERIALS

- Nylon paintbrush: 6" flat

- Flat latex paints: gold, taupe, white

- Synthetic sponge

WHAT TO DO

• Step 1: Sparingly load one side of a paintbrush with gold paint. In a vertical motion, lightly drag the paint down the wall, beginning at the top of the wall and continuing to the floor. This layer is randomly applied over the base coat allowing portions of the base coat color to show through. Repeat the dragging process. Working in 4' sections allows the following layers to mix with the coat of gold before the paint has completely dried.

• Step 2: Repeat Step 1 with taupe paint, allowing portions of all previous layers of paint to show through. Do not let paint dry completely.

• Step 3: Using a damp sponge, apply white paint in a circular rubbing motion over the entire wall to soften and blend the colors as desired. Let dry.

• Step 4: Repeat Step 3 as many times as necessary until the coats of gold and taupe are barely visible. Let dry.

• Step 5: Faux cracks may be added to the wall if desired. See Weathered Wood & Marble on page 40.

COFFEE TABLE

Just about everyone has a table lurking somewhere around their house that can't seem to find a "home." This was such a table.

The wood was in need of refinishing, but it had good structure. In order to accentuate its best features, I sanded away the dark stain and varnish in selected areas to reveal the raw wood underneath.

MATERIALS

- Coffee table
- 100-grit sandpaper
- Synthetic sponges
- Craft paints: metallic gold, verdigris, off-white
- Foam brush: 1" flat
- Satin acrylic sealer

WHAT TO DO

- Step 1: Sand the tabletop and selected areas of the table to accentuate its outstanding features and wipe clean.
- Step 2: Using a damp sponge, randomly sponge metallic gold paint onto the tabletop. Let dry.
- Step 3: Using a foam brush, paint stripes on the tabletop with verdigris paint. Let dry.
- Step 4: Using a dry sponge, randomly sponge off-white paint over the previous coats of paint. Do not let paint dry completely.
- Step 5: Using a damp sponge, slightly rub the coat of off-white, smearing and blending it into the previous coats of paint. Let dry.
- Step 6: Using the foam brush, seal the table. Let dry.

DECORATING TIPS

- If stripes are not your pattern of choice, try using different shapes such as diamonds or triangles. Wavy lines add a touch of whimsy.
- Free-form or stenciled lettering can have a big impact on this application. If you don't feel confident painting a pattern free-form, a wide variety of stencils are available.
- As an alternative to refinishing, this technique may be used on any paintable surface that is already weathered.

FORMAL
LIVING ROOM

WEATHERED WOOD & MARBLE

In this room, the "need" inspired the invention. The entire living room had been painted in a very formal mood. Elderberry burgundy was the color of the walls and high-gloss white had been used for all of the woodwork. Even though the look was elegant, it lacked the personality and character that reflected the way our family truly lived. We frequently met in this room for family gatherings and it was missing the comfortable casual elegance it needed.

I love the warm and weathered surfaces and textures that grace the homes of Europe. To me, the aged look is one of stability and comfort. It offers a serene and timeless ambience to any room. By adding "instant age" to the walls and woodwork, the cozy warmth I was looking for was created. At night, when we are together in this room, it literally glows.

MATERIALS FOR WEATHERED WOOD WALLS

- 100-grit sandpaper
- Paint roller & pan
- Flat latex paint: your choice of brown, burgundy, forest green, or dark taupe*

- Nylon paintbrush: 6" flat
- Flat latex paints: amber, light taupe, white
- Synthetic sponge

*Before purchasing your paint, check the clearance paints that have been mixed incorrectly to see if you can find a suitable color.

MATERIALS FOR FAUX CRACKS & KNOTS

- Craft paints: amber, brown, terra-cotta
- Nylon paintbrushes: #2 round, $1/4$" flat
- Synthetic sponge

WHAT TO DO

• Step 1: Lightly sand the surfaces to be painted and wipe clean.

• Step 2: Using a paint roller, apply a base coat of dark latex paint (brown, burgundy, forest green, or dark taupe) onto the walls, moldings, and woodwork. There is no need to completely cover the surfaces because additional applications will be added. Let dry.

STEP 2

• Step 3: Sparingly load one side of a 6" flat paintbrush with amber latex paint. In a vertical motion, lightly drag the paint down the wall, beginning at the top of the wall and continuing to the floor. This layer is randomly applied over the base coat, allowing portions of the base coat color to show through. Repeat the dragging process. Working in 4' sections allows the following layers to mix with the coat of amber before the paint has completely dried.

Continued on page 38.

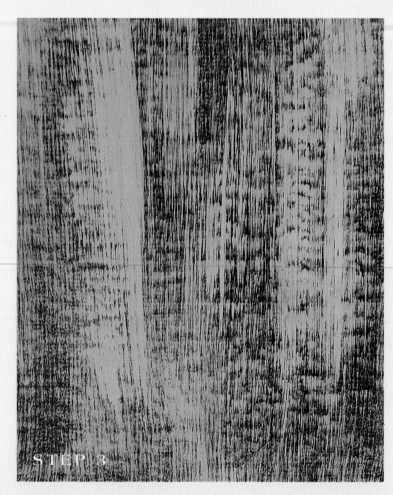

STEP 3

Continued from page 36.

• Step 4: Repeat Step 3 with light taupe latex paint, allowing portions of all previous layers of paint to show through. Do not let paint dry completely.

• Step 5: Using a damp sponge, gently drag over the layers of paint to blend the colors as desired. Do not let paint dry completely.

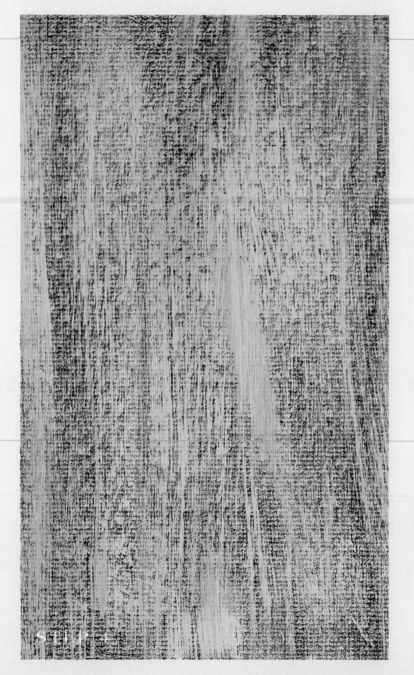

STEP 4

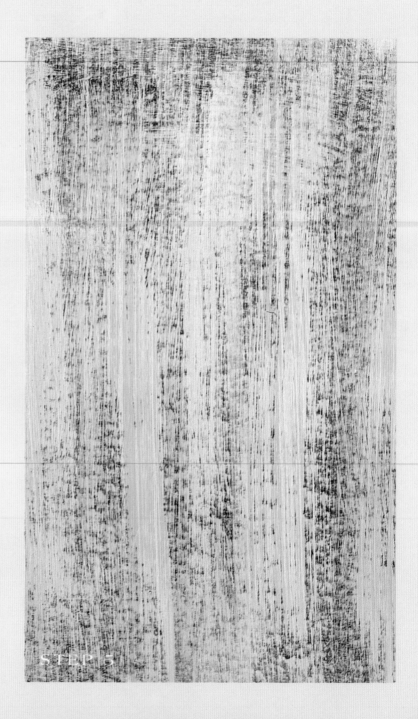

STEP 5

• Step 6: Repeat Step 3 with white latex paint, allowing portions of all previous layers of paint to show through. In addition to dragging the white paint onto the walls, pounce the paintbrush over the layers of paint in a random pattern. Do not let paint dry completely.

Continued on page 40.

Continued from page 39.

• Step 7: Repeat Step 5. Let dry.

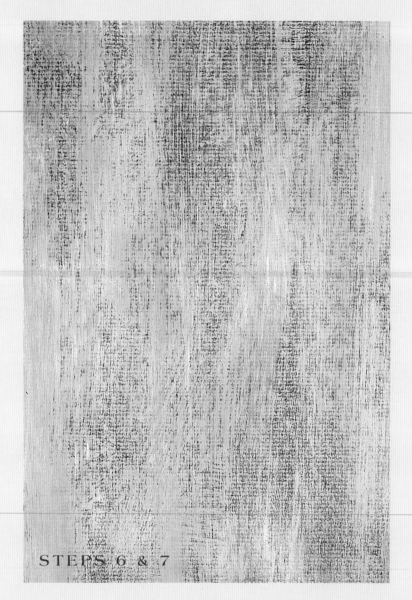

STEPS 6 & 7

• Step 8: Repeat Steps 3–7 for the moldings and woodwork. However, drag these areas in a horizontal pattern to create a contrasting marble effect.

• Step 9 (creating faux cracks): Dilute brown craft paint with a small amount of water. Dip a #2 round paintbrush into the diluted brown paint. In a serpentine motion, moving vertically, twist the paintbrush with your wrist to add "cracks" in varied widths. Using a ¼" flat paintbrush, immediately go back along the edges of the cracks, blurring the paint and leaving only fine lines resembling cracks. Let dry.

STEP 9

• Step 10 (creating faux knots): Dip the #2 round paintbrush into the diluted brown paint. Twist the paintbrush in an oblong pattern and spiral inward to the center of the "knot." Using the ¼" flat paintbrush, slightly blur all the lines downward by dragging the paintbrush over the spirals. Let dry.

• Step 11: Mix the amber and terra-cotta craft paints into a peach shade. Dilute the paint mixture with a small amount of water. Using a damp sponge, lightly apply the peach wash over the walls, moldings, and wood-work to unify the colors and give the wood a warm glow.

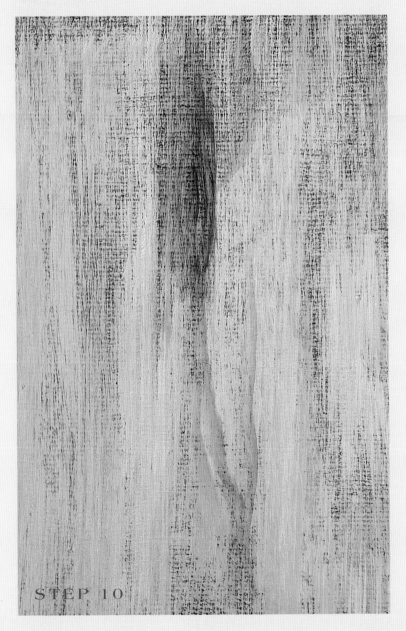

STEP 10

STEP 11

CHAINED PARLOR MIRRORS

These mirrors were purchased at a yard sale for 50¢ each. They were gold plastic and were made to hang vertically.

I painted them with black spray paint, leaving a touch of gold at each corner, and hot-glued a small shell to the top of each frame. A piece of chain, purchased at the hardware store, was installed to the back of the frames so they would hang horizontally. I hung them from brass drapery tie-backs.

The total cost was under $5 each.

MIRRORED MOSAIC FRAME

This frame was purchased at a thrift store for $5 and I had a lot of fun embellishing it.

It had an old velvet matting on the inside edge next to the wood. I purchased precut mirrored tiles at the local craft store and adhered them to the soiled velvet with jewelry glue to create a mosaic effect.

Gold beading was then used as an edge trim for the mirrored tiles and seashells were glued to each corner of the frame. The relief elements at the top of the frame are thrift-store finds that I applied with industrial-strength adhesive.

The faux gold wire is standard speaker wire from the local hardware store that was twisted and painted. It is secured to the frame with screws. The top arches of wire are secured in the floral-foam-anchored arrangement.

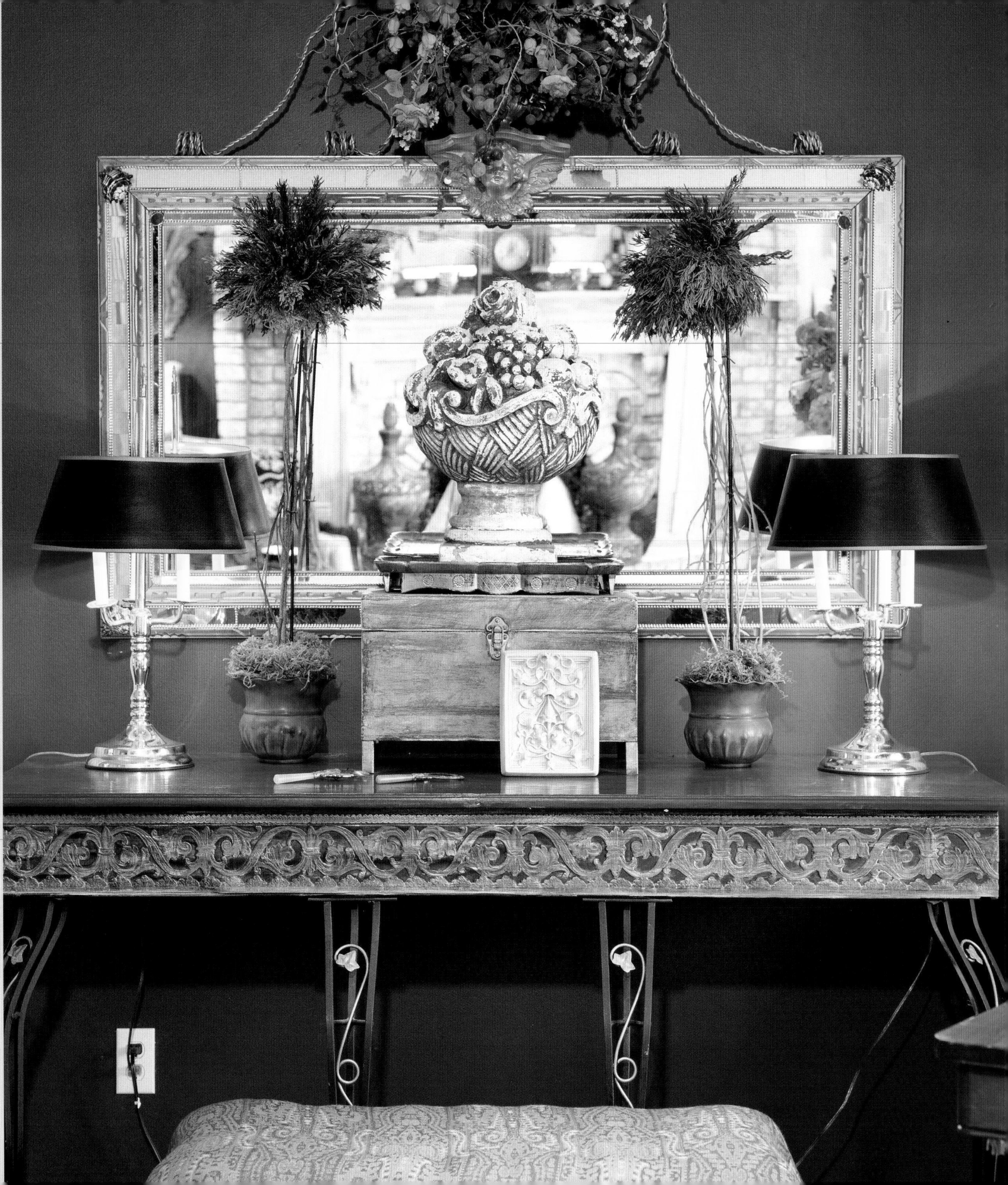

EMBOSSED COPPER TABLE

This console table is an easy and inexpensive way to add display surface for "tablescaping" and architectural interest to a room.

The dramatic faux embossed copper apron is the focal point of the table. It was created using embossed wallpaper border.

The legs that were used had been attached to a wrought-iron patio table that I acquired at a thrift-store for $10.

MATERIALS

- Oak-veneered plywood: 4' x 8' sheet

- Router & bit

- 200-grit sandpaper

- Standard lumber:
  2" x 4" x 6', 3 lengths
  2" x 2" x 4', 1 length

- Wood screws: 3"

- Construction adhesive

- Embossed wallpaper border: 4"-wide roll

- Nylon paintbrush: 2" flat

- Craft paints: black, metallic copper, verdigris

- Foam brush: 2" flat

- Stain: red mahogany

- High-gloss acrylic polyurethane sealer

- 4 Table legs: any height

WHAT TO DO

- Step 1: Cut the sheet of plywood to the desired dimensions or have your local lumber supplier precut it for you.

- Step 2: To create a finished edge, route the front and side edges with a router and the desired bit.

If preferred, edge molding can be added with finishing nails to create a decorative edge.

- Step 3: Lightly sand the top and the sides until smooth and wipe clean.

- Step 4: To make the table apron, cut the lengths of 2" x 4" to form a three-sided box. The box should be cut to allow a 2" recess under

STEP 8

STEP 9

the tabletop. Assemble the box with wood screws.

• Step 5: Place the plywood tabletop on top of the box (or apron) and adhere them together with construction adhesive to make a table. Allow for a 2" overhang on the front and both sides. Let dry.

• Step 6: Measure and cut the embossed wallpaper border to fit around the front and sides of the table apron.

• Step 7: Lay the wallpaper border flat. Using a paintbrush, apply a base coat of black paint onto the border. Let dry.

• Step 8: Using a foam brush, apply metallic copper paint onto the embossed areas of the border over the coat of black. Let dry.

• Step 9: Using the foam brush, lightly drag verdigris paint onto the embossed areas of the border over the coat of metallic copper. Let dry.

• Step 10: Install the wallpaper border on the front and sides of the table apron.

• Step 11: Stain the tabletop, following manufacturer's instructions. Let dry.

• Step 12: Using the paintbrush, seal the tabletop and the table apron. Let dry.

• Step 13: Lay the tabletop with the attached apron upside down on a padded surface to prevent scratching. Attach the legs, evenly spaced, along the front bottom edge of the table apron.

• Step 14: Position the table against the wall where it will be mounted. Mark the height just under the back edge of the table apron.

• Step 15: Cut the 2" x 2" to fit along the back edge of the table apron. Use the markings made in Step 14 to align the 2" x 2". Secure it to the wall studs with wood screws.

• Step 16: Set the table with legs attached on the 2" x 2" lip and secure it to the back bottom edge of the table apron with construction adhesive. Let dry.

This mirrored mosaic frame is the perfect choice for the chosen print. The technique used to embellish this frame is the same one de-scribed for the Mirrored Mosaic Frame on page 45.

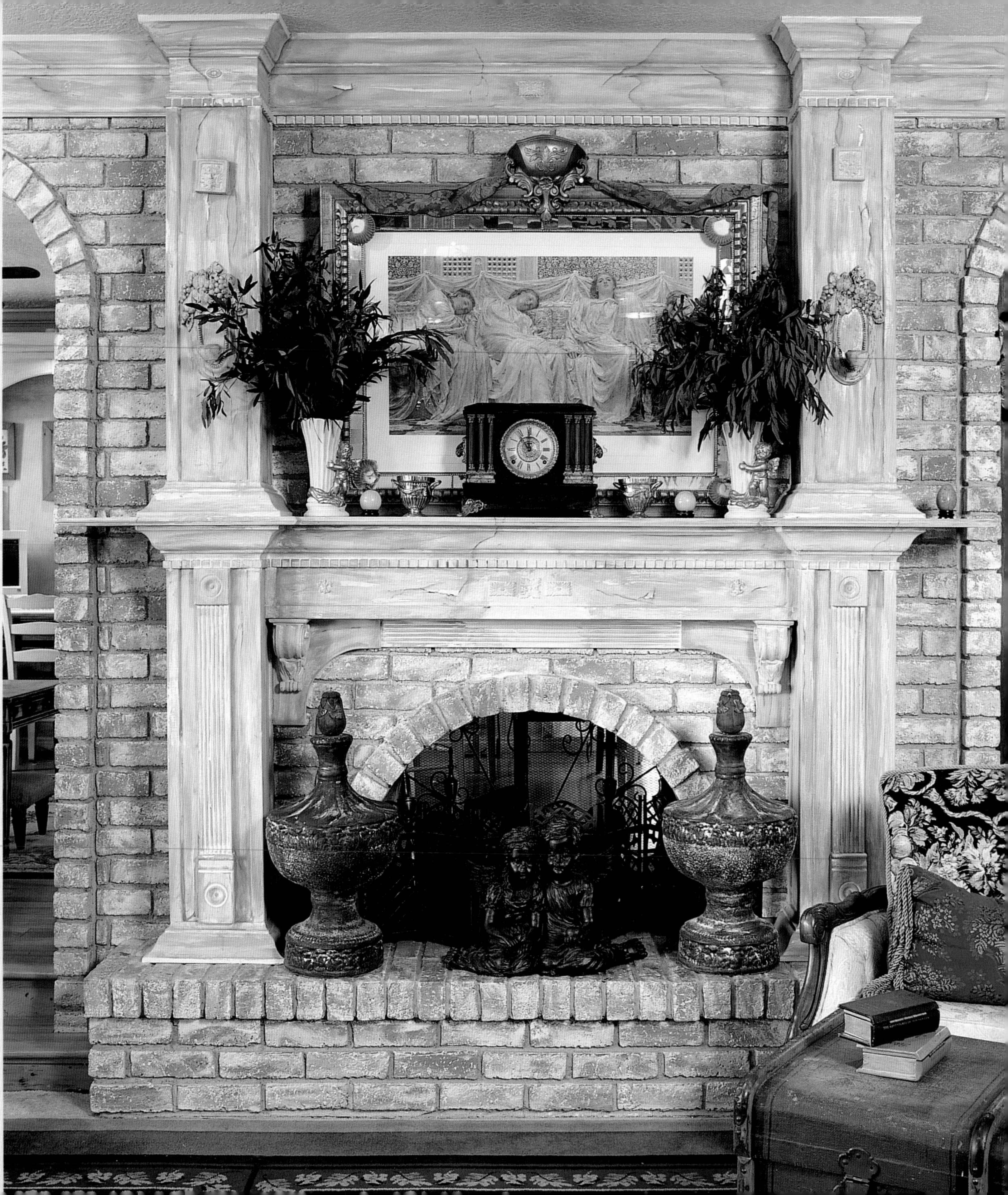

FIREPLACE MANTLE

My husband's ingenuity and willingness to accommodate my wild ideas came through once again on this fireplace mantle—it is nothing more than a series of 1" x 10" pine boxes dressed with add-ons and molding, then painted to look like the weathered wood walls in the living room.

The pine boxes were secured to previously attached 2" x 8" studs. The add-ons were applied with construction adhesive and the moldings were added with finishing nails. The entire mantle was caulked with paintable acrylic latex caulk, then painted.

LAMP BASE FINIALS

No one believes me when I tell them these amazing finials are actually old lamps purchased at a thrift store.

They are wonderful used in the house or in the garden. The crown on top is a glass pear purchased at a local discount store for $1. It was secured with construction adhesive.

MATERIALS

- Finial-shaped lamps

- 100-grit sandpaper

- Spray paint: black

- Synthetic sponge

- Craft paints: black, brown, metallic copper

- Glass pear adornments

51

- Construction adhesive
- White flour or spackling powder
- Spray bottle of water
- Satin acrylic spray sealer

WHAT TO DO

• Step 1: Strip the lamps of their electrical components.

• Step 2: Lightly sand the lamp bases to create a textured surface that will allow the spray paint to adhere, then wipe clean.

• Step 3: Paint the lamp bases with black spray paint. Let dry.

• Step 4: Using a damp sponge, randomly sponge brown craft paint onto the lamp bases over the coat of black. Let dry.

STEP 4

• Step 5: Randomly sponge metallic copper craft paint onto the lamp bases over the coat of brown. Let dry.

STEP 5

• Step 6: Randomly sponge black craft paint onto the lamp bases over the coat of metallic copper. Let dry.

STEP 6

- Step 7: Adhere the glass pear adornments to the top of the lamp bases with construction adhesive. Let dry.

- Step 8: Randomly sprinkle white flour over the finials, allowing the flour to settle in the crevices. Mist the flour with a spray bottle of water. Let dry. The flour sets into a paste and hardens as it dries. This provides the aging effect. Brush off excess flour. Additional coats of flour may be added as desired.

- Step 9: Using a spray sealer, seal the finials. Let dry.

- Step 10: Additional coats of sealer must be applied if the lamp base finials are to be displayed outdoors. Let dry between each coat.

DECORATING TIP

- Place a lamp base finial atop a concrete column and paint it to match. They make stunning garden sculptures.

FIREPLACE BRICKS

These bricks were once the perfect shade of dirty white. They begged for a major overhaul.

I love the old, used bricks that are being recycled into new construction projects, so I took a recycled brick with me to the craft store to match the paint colors.

Craft paint became the star in this transformation! The paint soaks into the brick making them washable, yet beautiful.

What could be easier? I painted these bricks and have not done any touch-up painting since they were finished seven years ago.

MATERIALS

- Brick wall or fireplace face
- Nylon paintbrush: 6" flat
- Craft paints: gray, dark mauve, light mauve, white
- Synthetic sponge

WHAT TO DO

- Step 1: Before beginning, clean the brick with hot water and a mild detergent.

- Step 2: Using a paintbrush, apply a base coat of dark mauve paint onto the surface of the bricks. Do not paint the edges of the bricks or the grout in between the bricks. Let dry.

- Step 3: Using a damp sponge, randomly sponge light mauve paint onto the bricks over the coat of dark mauve. Let dry.

- Step 4: Using the damp sponge, randomly sponge white paint onto the bricks over the coat of light mauve. Let dry.

- Step 5: Using the damp sponge, randomly "wipe" gray paint onto a few of the bricks over the coat of white. Make certain the finished look is balanced. Let dry.

- Step 6: To make the bricks look old and weathered, randomly sponge the very most raised surfaces of the bricks with white paint.

GREEN MIRROR

I found this beauty at the thrift store for $10. It was in excellent condition, except for a few areas on the border that were missing some antique gold leafing.

I decided to leave some of these areas untouched to promote the distressed effect I was looking for. I filled the remaining areas with gold leafing. This technique is done by rubbing the gold leafing on with your finger, which allows great control for distribution.

The mirror now looks as good as new—or should I say old! The furniture piece under the mirror is an antique sewing machine and cabinet, purchased at a thrift store for $15.

57

57

GLUE-GUN-UPHOLSTERED CHAIRS

This could well be the most re-warding of all the projects in this book! With the magic of your glue gun and some fabric, you can transform your outdated and worn pieces of furniture into personal expressions. Your imagination should kick into high gear as you discover the endless possibilities all around your home.

The chairs I used were rescued from a biannual neighborhood trash pick-up. Covered in snow, they needed a few days to dry out.

The wood was in need of either refinishing or painting. I opted for paint to accentuate the detailing on the arms and legs.

The fabric I used was a Mrs. Santa Claus skirt purchased from the thrift store for $3. I divided the fabric in half and decided what I would cover on the chairs. Because there would be a shortage, I purchased a remnant of green crushed velvet to complete the backs of the chairs.

The gold tassels and cording were purchased from a craft store. The 25' roll of cording was marked down to $5.99 on a Christmas clearance table.

These chairs have been glue-gun-upholstered for seven years and have survived six very active children and an assortment of cats and dogs. They continue to hold up beautifully. Because the hot glue fuses the old and new fabrics together, this technique holds up just as well as traditional upholstery methods.

MATERIALS

- Old upholstered chairs
- Fabric
- Hot-glue gun & glue sticks
- Scissors or craft knife
- Cording
- Transparent tape
- Tassels
- Upholstery thread

WHAT TO DO

• Step 1 (measuring fabric): Measure all areas of the chair that are currently upholstered. Add an additional 3" on all edges to allow for pulling and gluing.

• Step 2 (upholstering chair seat): Cut a piece of fabric and drape it over the chair seat so the seat is completely covered. If necessary, press the fabric to remove the wrinkles. Begin covering the chair seat by applying hot glue to the front, bottom edge of the chair seat. Apply the edge of the new piece of fabric to the glue. Once the front edge has fused, pull the fabric and hot-glue the back, bottom edge in place. Glue any excess fabric under the seat—do not let it hang down and be visible.

• Step 3 (upholstering front side of chair back): Begin covering the front side of the chair back by applying hot glue to the top edge of the chair back. Drape the fabric to allow a 3" overhang—this will eventually be trimmed away.

If there are tufts in the chair, apply the hot glue directly into the crevices of the existing tufts. Drape the fabric over the chair front and, using a butter knife, push the new fabric into the crevices. Apply the hot glue one crevice at a time, allowing the fabric to be manipulated correctly.

After the entire front of the chair has been re-upholstered, use scissors or a sharp craft knife to trim away all excess fabric. Make certain to trim evenly with the existing edge of the chair where the fabric on the front of the chair ends and the fabric for the back of the chair will begin.

• Step 4 (upholstering back side of chair back): Begin covering the back side of the chair back by applying hot glue to the top edge of the chair back. Drape the fabric to allow for a 3" over-hang—this will eventually be trimmed away. The back and front edges of the newly upholstered fabric should be touching.

To alleviate wrinkling, pull the fabric around the edges of the chair back and pull taut. After the entire back of the chair has been reupholstered, trim all ex-cess fabric away.

• Step 5 (trimming edges with cording): It is necessary to trim all of the edges to cover up the hot-glued seams. Begin on the back, bottom edge of the chair seat. Working in small sec-tions, start applying hot glue directly along the bottom edge of the chair. Immedi-ately apply the cording over the glue. When you need to cut the cording, place a piece of transparent tape on it where it is to be cut. Make the cut on the oppo-site side of the tape. The end that will be glued down will retain the tape and help prevent it from fraying. After the hot glue is dry, the tape can be removed.

Hot-glue the cording around all of the edges where the excess fabric has been trimmed away. This creates an instant finished edge—simulating traditional cording and hiding all the seams.

• Step 6 (adding tassels): If you are using tassels, secure them with upholstery thread.

DECORATING TIPS

• Tackle a sofa using this same technique.

• Use contrasting fabrics that you get as remnant pieces and tie the look together with pillows made from all of the different fabrics.

• Collect remnant pieces of fabric and trim in the colors you like—try to buy at least two yards at a time.

LAMP BASE STILL LIFE

This stunning statue was once the base of a lamp. I purchased the old lamp at a thrift store for $10, brought it home, and removed all of the electrical components.

I then put it out in my garden and let the painted exterior weather naturally. When it had the patina I desired, I brought it back inside.

This lamp base still life has become one of my favorite pieces. Because of its large scale, it makes a wonderful center-piece for tablescaping.

Similar concrete still lifes can also be purchased and painted. When the painted piece is left outdoors for two to three weeks, the paint will weather to a pleasing patina.

WEATHERED WOOD BOXES

Any wooden box can be used to achieve this effect. It is simply a series of paint layers applied on top of one another and lightly sanded in selected areas between layers.

These weathered wood boxes make a wonderful accent piece for enhancing other accessories or standing alone in the spotlight.

Using boxes such as these is a great way to stretch your decorating resources—they can be moved from room to room to create an entirely different impact in each room they are displayed.

Using different colors of craft paint is also a great way to add interest and dimension to any room in your home.

MATERIALS

- Wooden box

- Nylon paintbrush: 6" flat

- Craft paints: light mauve, wheat, off-white

- 100-grit sandpaper

- Synthetic sponge

- White vinegar

WHAT TO DO

• Step 1: Using a paintbrush, apply a base coat of off-white paint onto the entire box. Let dry.

• Step 2: Lightly sand off some of the paint, allowing portions of the wood to show through.

• Step 3: Using the paintbrush, lightly apply a coat of light mauve paint. Let dry.

• Step 4: Lightly sand off some of the light mauve paint, allowing portions of the off-white layer to show through.

Continued on page 67.

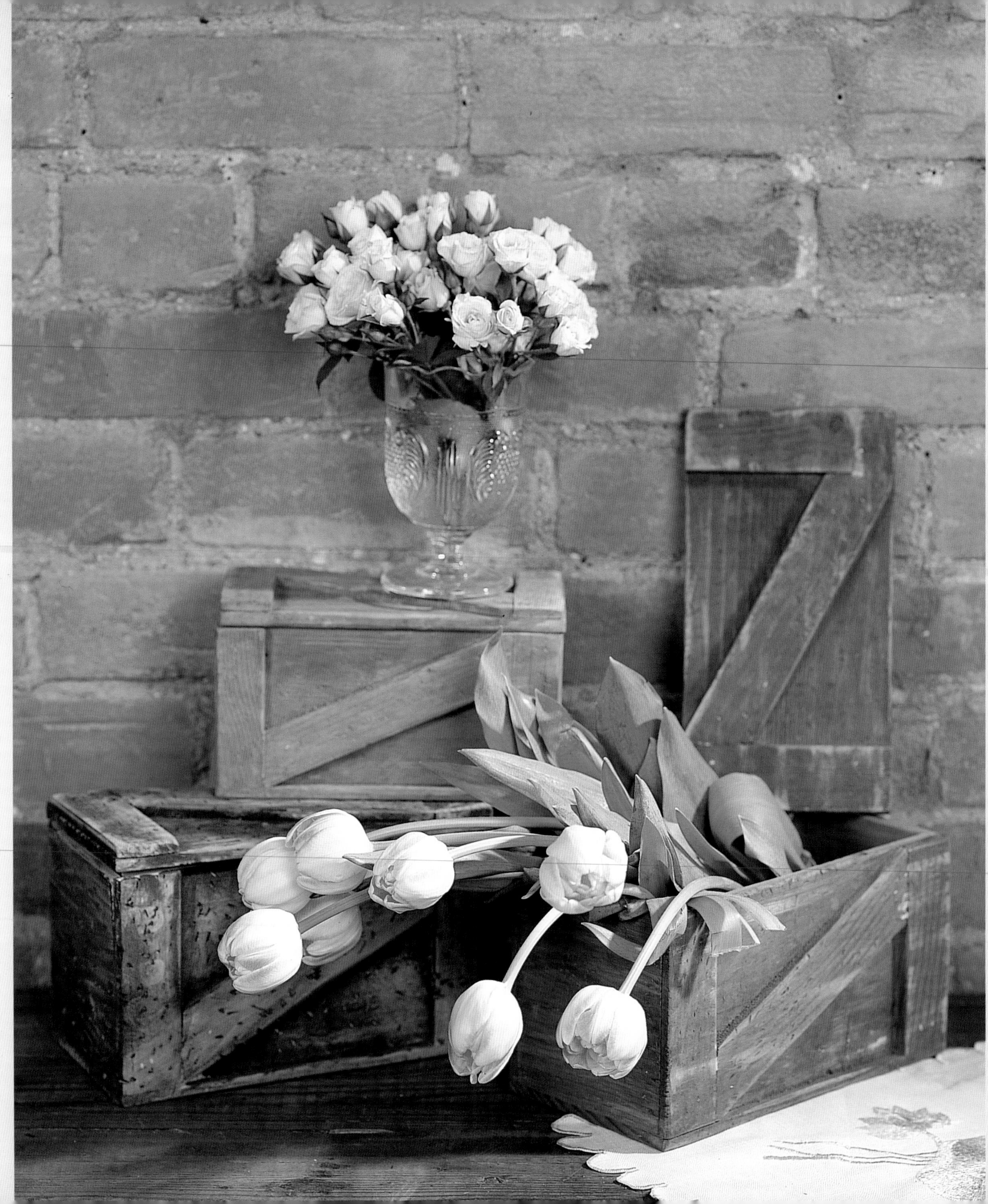

Continued from page 65.

• Step 5: Using the paintbrush, lightly apply a coat of wheat paint. Let dry.

• Step 6: Lightly sand off some of the wheat paint, allowing portions of all previous layers of paint to show through. Let dry.

• Step 7: Sprinkle white vinegar over the top of the box and let it sit on the wood until the paint visibly begins to bubble.

• Step 8: Using a dry sponge, wipe over the top of the box to clean and blend the bubbled paint. Let dry.

STEP 6

STEPS 7 & 8

• Step 9: Repeat Steps 7–8 for the sides of the box.

FAUX COPPER VERDIGRIS VASE

This vase had great form, but the original colors were hideous! It was rescued from the thrift store for $2.

I found some copper paint with real copper crystals and the verdigris finish at the craft store. The finish is a clear liquid that reacts with real copper crystals, creating an actual verdigris finish. This finish really fit with the Grecian feel of the vase.

It quickly became one of my husband's favorite accent pieces.

MATERIALS

- Vase
- 100-grit sandpaper
- Foam brush: 2" flat
- Copper paint containing copper crystals
- Verdigris finish for copper paint

WHAT TO DO

- Step 1: Lightly sand the vase and wipe clean.
- Step 2: Using a foam brush, apply two or three coats of copper paint onto the vase. Let dry between each coat.
- Step 3: Using the foam brush, apply the verdigris finish to the copper around the upper rim of the vase and let it "drizzle" down the vase. This will create the look of oxidized copper. The copper paint will turn green as the finish dries.
- Step 4: Additional coats of verdigris finish may be added for a more dramatic oxidizing effect.

DECORATING TIPS

- Many of the glass or plaster decor items found at thrift stores have been discarded due to outdated colors. Use this technique to give them a "timeless" patina.
- Try this method on old drawer handles for a dramatic effect.

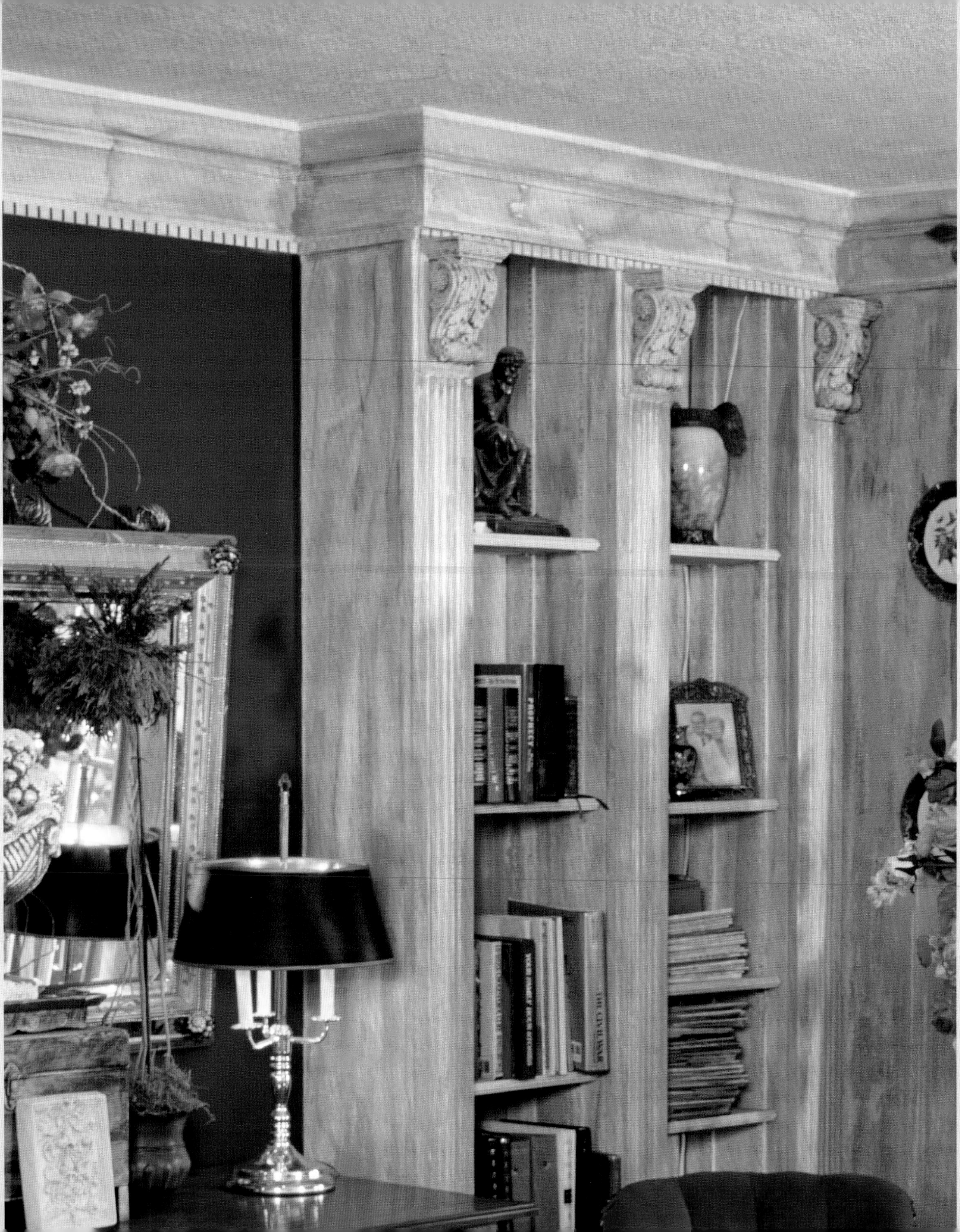

FAUX WOOD BRACKETS

For approximately $8, you can add instant architecture to any space in your home. These plaster brackets can be purchased at any craft store and will adhere easily to any wall with construction adhesive or finishing nails. They can be painted with any technique and will transport the plain to palatial!

MATERIALS

- Plaster brackets
- Construction adhesive
- Paintable acrylic latex caulk
- Latex paint

WHAT TO DO

- Step 1: Determine where you want to place each bracket.

- Step 2: Place a small amount of construction adhesive on the back of the first bracket.

- Step 3: Push the bracket into place, then pull it away leaving some of the construction adhesive on the wall. Let it dry to the touch —it must still be wet underneath.

- Step 4: Push the bracket back into position and hold it in place, making certain it does not slip. When it is secure, without any chance of slipping, let go. Let dry for at least one hour before beginning to paint.

- Step 5: Repeat Steps 2–4 for each bracket.

- Step 6: Caulk all the edges around each bracket. Let dry.

- Step 7: Paint the brackets as desired. Let dry.

TABLE WITH FAUX GOLD WIRE

This mahogany table was in pieces in the garbage behind my favorite thrift store—even they didn't see any value in it!

I brought it home and pieced it together. The bottom was missing one of the gold foot caps so I sponged the entire base with metallic gold craft paint to disguise the missing piece. The metallic gold paint became the inspiration for the faux gold wiring that I added to the table apron and draped through drawer pulls.

MATERIALS

- Table with apron

- Drawer pulls

- Drill & bit

- Standard electrical wire: any gauge

- Spray paint: gold

- Wire cutters

- Craft wire

WHAT TO DO

- Step 1: Space the drawer pulls evenly around the table apron and mark placement for drilling.

- Step 2: Drill the holes in the table apron to accommodate the size of the screws on the drawer pulls.

- Step 3: Install the drawer pulls.

- Step 4: Twist the electrical wire until it is the length needed for draping around the table apron as desired.

- Step 5: Paint the twisted electrical wire with gold spray paint. Let dry.

- Step 6: To make each tassel, fold electrical wire back and forth several times and cut it on the ends with wire cutters. Secure the strands with craft wire.

- Step 7: Paint the tassels with gold spray paint. Let dry.

- Step 8: Drape the twisted wire through the drawer pulls, folding the end of the wire around the last drawer pull.

- Step 9: Secure the tassels to the drawer pulls with craft wire.

WALL SCONCES

These wonderful plastic sculptures are sure to be lurking in a thrift store near you! I have boxes and boxes of these treasures— some that I have acquired for as little as 25¢.

You might be wondering why anyone would want boxes of these, but I have pulled out the boxes time and time again when creating wall sculptures for our home.

Because they are lightweight, they are easy to hang and they create instant architecture at less than a fraction of the cost of plaster or wood add-ons. In addition, they take paint beautifully, allowing an easy transformation to faux marble, wood, stone, or plaster.

MATERIALS

- Plastic sconces
- Finishing nails
- Paintable acrylic latex caulk
- Latex paint
- Foam brush: 2" flat

WHAT TO DO

- Step 1: Determine where you want to place each sconce.

- Step 2: Hang the sconces with finishing nails.

- Step 3: Caulk all the edges around each sconce. Let dry.

- Step 4: Paint the sconces as desired. Let dry.

DECORATING TIP

- Battery-operated candles can be inserted into the sconce and a lamp shade added to create a small wall lamp.

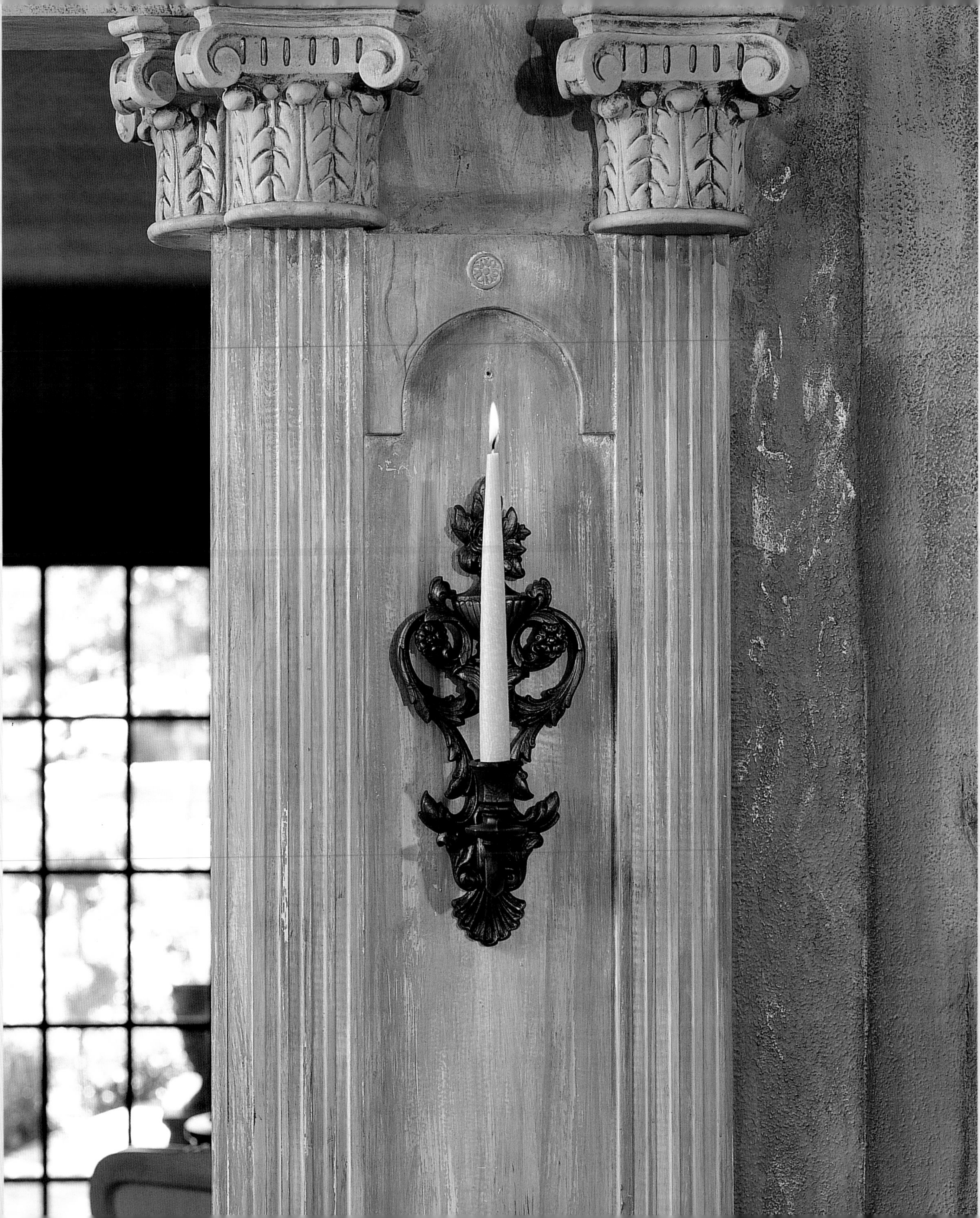

TABLE LAMPS

These lamps were purchased for $5 each. The bases were Mediterranean gold-toned and the lamp shades were 3' tall and 2' wide. They were not to my liking, but the form was there; so I snatched them up and put a fresh coat of pewter paint on them. I applied silver leafing to the raised surfaces and purchased new lamp shades. They were perfect on the table behind the sofa.

TRUNK TABLE

Here is a great way to recycle that old trunk into a new life. Add legs to the bottom and presto, you have a trunk table!

The legs on this thrift-store find were part of another thrift-store table. I cut the spindles in half and secured them onto the bottom of the trunk from the inside with 3" wood screws.

The rustic finish adds warmth and contrast to the other more classic furnishings in the room.

DECORATING TIP

• Fence post sculptures may be installed to the bottom of a trunk to simulate legs.

ENTRY & HALLWAYS

ENTRY

The faux marble column entrance into the living room adds importance to this otherwise plain transition. Existing wall corners were used for the fluted columns, and plaster brackets form the caps to the columns. The fluting and brackets were installed with construction adhesive and all of the edges were caulked with paintable acrylic latex caulk.

The faux marble cross beam was painted in the same colors and horizontal dragging method as the living room. The edges were shaded to provide dimension. The adornment in the center is an independent piece hung with a finishing nail to the existing crown molding. Any doorway or room transition could benefit from this treatment—instant architecture for pennies!

DECORATING TIP

• Crown molding can be used for the column crown instead of the plaster brackets.

CUPBOARD DOOR PANELING

In making my daily trek to the thrift store, I found these wonderful solid oak panels that are actually cupboard doors. They jumped out at me and yelled, "take me home!" Priced at only $3 each, I couldn't resist, even though I had no idea what I was going to do with them.

I brought them into the house and for lack of a better place to store them, I set them in the entry against the wall. I left for the market and when I returned, I walked in the front door and immediately caught the vision of using the doors as wall paneling, right where they were.

There weren't enough panels to cover the walls I wanted to panel, so I had to improvise. I spaced them out evenly across the walls and measured the space between them to ensure they were balanced.

I purchased a sheet of oak-veneered plywood and cut it into sections to fill the extra space between the panels. Chair rail was purchased to act as a cap for the paneling. I took one of the cupboard doors to the paint store and had them match the original stain color.

I stained the plywood sections and the chair rail to match the cupboard doors. The plywood sections were installed and the doors were placed over them to cover the edges and add another visual dimension to the faux paneling. The chair rail was installed above the doors and plywood strips to finish the top edges.

One wall in the entry was paneled as was one side of the entire length of the hallway.

You could say that this thrift-store find actually found the project!

SKY & CLOUD WALLS

This technique is so much easier than it looks. The beauty of it is that you can keep adding paint until you are happy with the results. This entire project was finished in a single day.

Try painting the sky and clouds on the ceiling or on a favorite piece of furniture.

MATERIALS

- Nylon paintbrush: 2" flat, 6" flat

- Craft paints: amber, powder blue, sky blue, teal, white

- Synthetic sponge

WHAT TO DO

You will need to begin on a wall that is painted white or off-white.

• Step 1: Using a 6" flat paintbrush, apply a small amount of teal paint along the top edge of the wall. Working from top to bottom, blend and fade the teal paint onto the wall as you continue downward. Let dry.

• Step 2: Using the paintbrush, blend a small amount of sky blue paint onto the bottom edge of the teal. Let dry.

• Step 3: Using the paintbrush, blend a small amount of powder blue paint onto the bottom edge of the sky blue. Do not let paint dry completely.

• Step 4: Using the paintbrush, randomly paint sections with white paint to create the bases for the clouds. Let dry.

• Step 5: Using the edge of the paintbrush and a pouncing motion, feather in the clouds with white paint over the top of the cloud bases. Blend with a horizontal stroke. Let dry.

• Step 6: Using a 2" flat paintbrush, feather a small amount of amber paint along the bottom edges of the clouds to simulate sunlight. Let dry.

• Step 7: Dilute white paint with a small amount of water. Using a damp sponge, lightly apply the white wash over the wall. Let dry.

Additional paint may be added for more intense color.

STEP 1

STEP 2

STEP 3

STEP 4

STEPS 5 & 6

VINEGAR-WEATHERED WOOD

This project was a spin-off of the weathered wood walls I painted in the living room. However, I wanted the walls in my entry, including the guest closet door, to be a little more dramatic, so I decided on a technique that offered more definition in the painted lines.

The closet door was high-gloss white, as was the previous finish on the living room woodwork, and now it didn't quite flow with the rest of the space. The easy solution was to paint it to match the weathered walls in the living room, but the undercoat of the living room was elderberry burgundy so it would have been a challenge to match the overall paint effect.

The entry walls had wallpaper, some of which had been installed over a damaged wall surface so it had to stay. Heavy paper, made for covering existing wallpaper, was applied over the wallpaper to act as a primer coat, providing a clean canvas to either repaper or paint. I decided to paint the walls and closely matched the elderberry burgundy as a base coat for the entry walls and closet door.

MATERIALS

- 100-grit sandpaper

- Paint roller & pan

- Flat latex paint: your choice of brown, burgundy, forest green, or dark taupe*

- Nylon paintbrush: 6" flat

- Flat latex paints: gold, light taupe, white

- Synthetic sponge

- White vinegar

*Before purchasing your paint, check the clearance paints that have been mixed incorrectly to see if you can find a suitable color.

Continued on page 92.

Continued from page 90.

WHAT TO DO

• Step 1: Lightly sand the surfaces to be painted and wipe clean.

If painting over wallpaper, there is no need to sand.

• Step 2: Using a paint roller, apply a base coat of dark latex paint (brown, burgundy, forest green, or dark taupe) onto the walls and closet door. There is no need to completely cover the surfaces because additional applications will be added. Let dry.

• Step 3: Sparingly load one side of a 6" flat paintbrush with gold latex paint. In a vertical motion, lightly drag the paint down the wall (and door), beginning at the top of the wall and continuing to the top of the chair rail or to the floor. This layer is randomly applied over the base coat, allowing portions of the base coat color to show through. Repeat the dragging process. Working in 4' sections allows the following layers to mix with the coat of gold before the paint has completely dried.

• Step 4: Repeat Step 3 with light taupe latex paint, allowing portions of all previous layers of paint to show through. Do not let paint dry completely.

• Step 5: Repeat Step 3 with white latex paint, allowing portions of all previous layers of paint to show through. Do not let paint dry completely.

• Step 6: Using a damp sponge, gently drag over the layers of paint to blend the colors as desired. Let dry.

• Step 7: Using the paintbrush, randomly apply white vinegar over the entry walls and closet door.

• Step 8: Using the damp sponge, wipe over the application of vinegar to partially reveal the elberberry burgundy layer and give the layers of paint a streaked appearance. Blend until the desired effect is achieved.

If too much paint is unintentionally removed, additional paint may be applied in the previously specified order.

DECORATING TIPS

• This technique, done with neutral colors, will simulate naturally-weathered pine.

• Outdated laminate countertops can be sanded, primed, and painted with this technique. With several coats of sealer, they will be durable, as well as beautiful.

• Soiled and/or outdated wallpaper can be sealed and painted using this method.

ENTRY CABINET

You can customize any piece of furniture with a little ingenuity and imagination! What once was a boring piece of antique furniture is now a one-of-a-kind piece of art.

Plaster still-life plaques, acquired at the junk store, were applied to the sides with construction adhesive and the edges were caulked with paintable acrylic latex caulk.

Wallpaper border was distressed for the top front sections and the edges were caulked. I took the botanical motif and custom-painted companion botanicals for the front insets. Brass wall ornaments were added to the bottom of the front and caulked. I painted

the swags and wheat sheaves and replaced the existing hardware with crystal knobs to give it additional sparkle and elegance.

I went over all of the edges with gold leafing.

The top of the cabinet was refinished and stained to match the original mahogany color.

This is my favorite piece because it has so much personality. One of my near-future projects will be to finish an antique mahogany secretary from the junk store as a companion piece to this cabinet.

DECORATING TIP

• Salvage old hardware from furniture that is beyond repair. Recycle it onto a new piece and add instant antiquity.

SECRET GARDEN HALLWAY WALL

This is one of my all-time favorite projects! The plastic add-ons, old discarded wooden cupboard doors, picture frames, and junk-store finds turned the walls of this long, boring hallway into a secret garden.

Any wall, large or small, could benefit from a Cinderella treatment like this. You could even do this to customize flat wooden doors all over your home.

MATERIALS

- Plastic add-ons
- Wooden cupboard doors
- Picture frames
- Medallions
- Clocks
- Wooden or polyfoam fluted molding
- Wooden or polyfoam end caps
- Construction adhesive
- Paintable acrylic latex caulk
- Nylon paintbrush: 6" flat
- Flat latex paint: stone gray
- Plastic grocery bags
- Craft paint: metallic pewter
- Synthetic sponge
- White flour or spackling powder
- Spray bottle of water

WHAT TO DO

- Step 1: Decide where you are going to place the decorative accessories (add-ons, cupboard doors, picture frames, etc.).

To help in designing a pattern, lay the collection of accessories on the floor and move them around until they are arranged the way you like them.

- Step 2: Adhere the arrangement onto the wall with construction adhesive.

Using a level, plumb line, and tape measure for symmetrical design will ensure that your accessories will be evenly spaced and hung straight.

Continued on page 97.

Continued from page 95.

- Step 3: Caulk all the edges around each decorative accessory. Let dry.

- Step 4: Using a paint-brush, apply a base coat of stone gray latex paint onto the accessories and the wall. Let dry.

- Step 5: Crinkle a plastic grocery bag and dip it into metallic pewter craft paint. Wipe off excess paint to avoid dripping.

- Step 6: Randomly "rag" over the top of the accessories and the wall. The metallic look of the pewter paint will contrast with the flat texture of the gray stone paint, giving a soft sheen. Let dry.

- Step 7: Using a damp sponge, lightly sponge along all of the edges of the raised elements on the accessories with the metallic pewter craft paint. Blend the edges into the existing ragged wall surface.

- Step 8: Gently throw white flour over the accessories, allowing the flour to settle in the crevices. Mist the flour with a spray bottle of water. Let dry. The flour sets into a paste and hardens as it dries. This provides the aging effect. Brush off excess flour. Additional coats of flour may be added as desired.

STEPS 2 & 3

STEPS 4–7

97

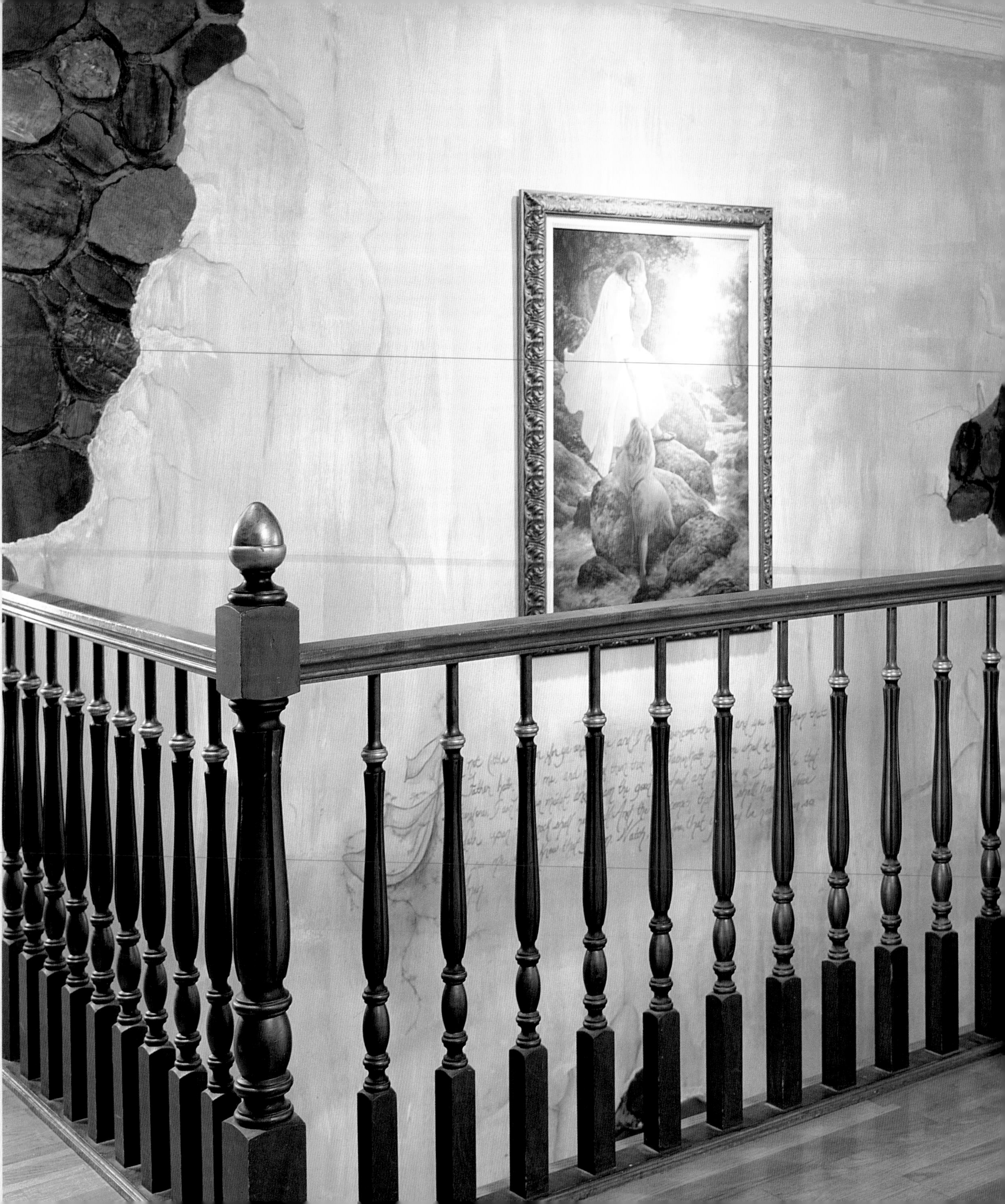

STAIR RAILS

This was an existing maple stair rail that looked dated and needed refinishing. I've always loved the look of metal railing, but it never seems to fit into the budget. After some experimenting, I found that craft manufacturers have created some wonderful, realistic metallic finishes that are believable copycats.

I sanded the stair rail, then painted the spindles, the base, and the finials with black green craft paint. It was important to get the paint into all of the crevices and grooves since these areas were to become part of the focal point of the finished project. After letting the paint dry completely, I applied a light coat of metallic pewter craft paint over the spindles, base, and finials. Finally, I painted all of the knobs on the spindles and the tops of the finials with metallic gold craft paint.

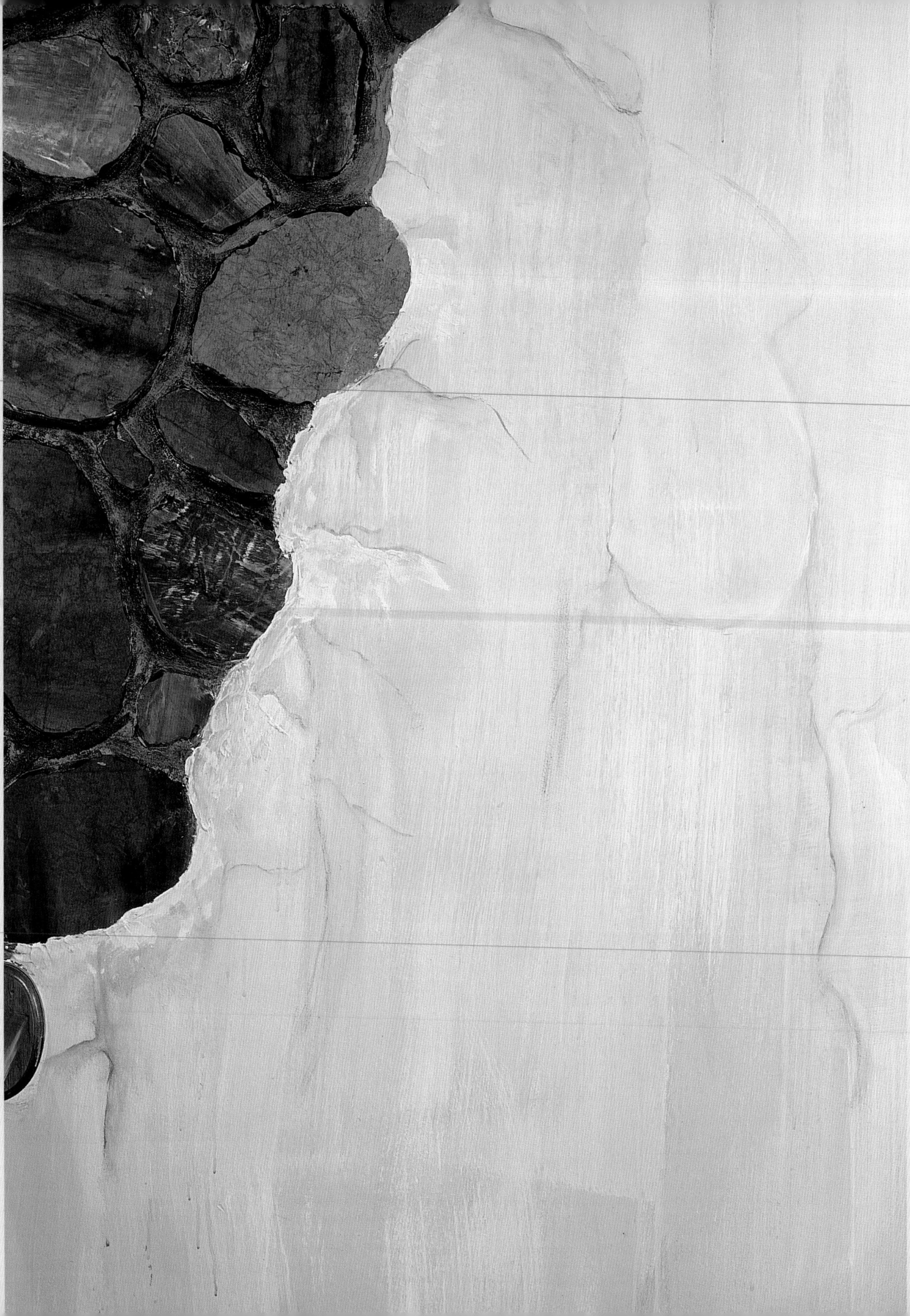

PAPER BAG ROCKS

This is a project a child could help you with. In fact, I actually had my kids help me paint the brown paper grocery bags used for the "rocks."

I got such a kick out of the response this project generated. People had to actually touch the rocks to satisfy their eyes that the rocks were not real. The faux mortar adds just enough texture to almost fool yourself!

By adding plaster to the wall around the rocks, the eye is fooled once again into believing the plaster has deteriorated away from the wall, revealing the rocks underneath.

MATERIALS FOR PAPER BAG ROCKS

- Brown paper grocery bags

- Nylon paintbrush: 6" flat

- Craft paints: black, brown, metallic pewter, taupe, white

- Synthetic sponge

MATERIALS FOR FAUX MORTAR

- Wallpaper paste: 1 quart

- All-purpose sand: 2 cups

- Craft paints: black, gray

- Putty knife

- Nylon paintbrush: $\frac{1}{4}$" flat

WHAT TO DO

Each brown paper grocery bag will yield four to six large rocks or ten to twelve small rocks.

- Step 1: Open each brown paper grocery bag and cut off the bottoms. Lay the bags flat with the printed side down.

- Step 2: Using a 6" flat paintbrush, randomly apply the black, brown, metallic pewter, taupe, and white paints over the entire surface of each bag, blending the colors into each other. Let dry.

- Step 3: Crinkle the painted bag, then open it and lay it as flat as possible.

• Step 4: Using a damp sponge, lightly rub the raised surfaces of the crinkled bags with white paint. Let dry.

• Step 5: Cut the painted bags into various rock shapes in a variety of sizes.

• Step 6: Position the "paper bag rocks" on the wall as desired and adhere with wallpaper paste. Make certain to leave an adequate amount of space between the rocks for the mortar. Let dry.

• Step 7: Mix 1 part all-purpose sand to 2 parts wallpaper paste to create the mortar, mixing in small increments so it does not dry out.

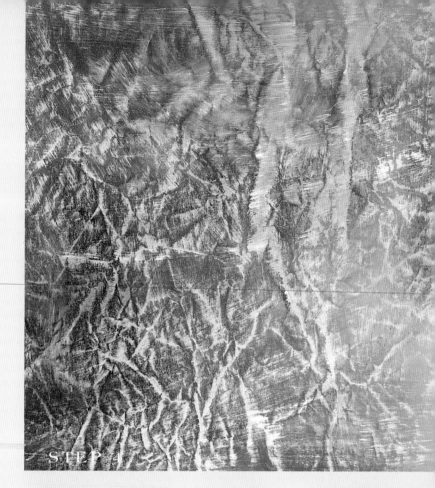

STEP 4

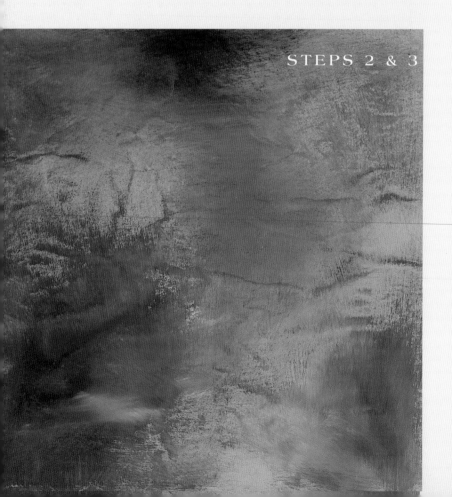

STEPS 2 & 3

STEPS 5 & 6

• Step 8: Add gray craft paint to the mixture until it is the desired shade. The mortar will dry 2–3 shades darker.

• Step 9: Using a putty knife, apply the mortar between the rocks on the wall. Make certain to add some mortar around each rock to cover all of the edges. Let dry.

• Step 10: Dilute black craft paint with a small amount of water. Using a $1/4$" flat paintbrush, paint shadows on each rock with the diluted black paint to add dimension. With the flat tip of the paintbrush, paint a fine line around the bottom edge of each rock. Wipe the paintbrush and go back over the edge, blending the line into the mortar.

The location of the shadows on the rocks can vary from rock to rock as long as the "light source" is coming from the same direction.

FAUX DISTRESSED PLASTER

Create a wonderful faux distressed plaster wall that complements the paper bag rocks and gives them somewhere to nestle. This layer of plaster renders valuable dimension. Additionally, the plaster wall is the perfect backdrop for the stair rail as it allows both to stand on their own and not compete with each other.

MATERIALS

• Putty knife

• Wallboard joint compound: 1 box

• Synthetic sponge

• Craft paints: cream, gold, white

WHAT TO DO

• Step 1: Using a putty knife, apply joint compound onto the wall in small sections. Overlap the edges of the rocks, leaving some of the edges raised. Smooth the joint compound away from the rocks onto the wall. Let dry.

• Step 2: Using a damp sponge, randomly sponge the cream and gold paints over the entire surface of the faux plaster, blending the colors into each other. Let dry.

• Step 3: Using the damp sponge, lightly rub the raised surfaces of the faux plaster with white paint. Let dry.

STEP 1

STEP 3

DECORATING TIPS

• This effect can be used on faux painted bricks as well.

• Create this deteriorating plaster effect in sections on a slightly contrasting colored wall. The resulting effect will be equally dramatic.

• Build-up the plaster in heavier layers and actually chip some away after it has been painted.

FRESCO CALLIGRAPHY

This is a great way to personalize your home! Choose a favorite saying, poem, verse, or short story to write on the wall. This happens to be a scripture that complements the painting by artist Greg Olson.

Practice what you want to write and the style in which you want to execute it on a piece of paper first. I chose to enlarge and embellish the first letter of the scripture, filling it in with a complementary color. I then painted a very faint vine entwined around it. This helps to draw the eye to the beginning of the verse.

MATERIALS

- Calligraphy pen: gold

- Craft paints: desired colors

- Synthetic sponge

- Flat latex paint: white

- White artist's eraser

WHAT TO DO

• Step 1: Using a #2 pencil, measure and mark lines for the text on the wall.

Using a level and tape measure will ensure that your lines will be evenly spaced and straight.

• Step 2: Lightly write the text on the wall.

• Step 3: Trace over the text with a gold calligraphy pen. Let dry.

• Step 4: Using a clean white eraser, erase the pencil lines and letters.

• Step 5: If desired, fill in the first letter of the verse with craft paint colors of your choice. Additional designs, such as the vine, should be drawn on and painted at this time. Let dry.

• Step 6: Dilute white latex paint with a small amount of water. Using a damp sponge, lightly apply the white wash over the verse. Let dry.

• Step 7: Additional applications of the white wash may be applied randomly to the verse, making it appear as though the "fresco calligraphy" is fading with age.

MASTER
BED & BATH

BRASS & COPPER CANOPY BED

This bed has provided much restful satisfaction! It creates the feel of romance that I gravitate to. It is an iron and brass bed that we purchased when I was expecting our third child. Rob was working at a furniture store so we got it at a discount. It was our first big retail purchase!

The bed was great and served its purpose well for the next 17 years and three more children. But one's taste changes, so I felt the bed was in need of an overhaul. Rob made small wooden risers for each bed leg. This was to serve a dual purpose. First, we are both tall and we wanted a tall bed. We wanted more height for added romance, but also as an obstacle for our two smallest boys who wanted to jump into bed with us in the middle of the night. Well, the second idea proved to be futile, but we did get our wish of a fairy-tale bed!

MATERIALS

- Brass bed with balls and posts on the head- and footboards
- Wood
- Pipe cutters
- Copper pipe: 1"
- Drapery clips
- 4 Copper pipe "T" fittings: 1"
- 4 Copper pipe 90° connector fittings: 1"
- Construction adhesive
- Muslin
- Fabric, optional
- 100-grit sandpaper
- Synthetic sponge
- Craft paints: black, brown, metallic copper
- Foam brush: 1" flat
- Satin acrylic sealer

WHAT TO DO

- Step 1: Remove the brass balls and posts from the head- and footboards. There must be a threaded metal rod under each post cover, as the canopy posts will slide over these and offer the support needed.

- Step 2: Measure and cut the wood for the risers to elevate the bed.

If desired, premanufactured risers can be installed.

- Step 3: Measure the desired height of the canopy. Using pipe cutters, cut the copper pipe into four equal lengths to make the canopy posts.

- Step 4: Measure the perimeter of the bed and cut the copper pipe into four sections to make the canopy frame.

- Step 5: Thread the desired number of drapery clips onto the four pieces of the canopy frame.

- Step 6: Attach the "T" fittings for the canopy posts onto each end of the two frame pieces that extend across the width of the bed.

- Step 7: Attach the 90° connector fittings onto the end of each frame section.

- Step 8: Attach all of the pieces together to make certain every piece fits together properly. When you are confident that all of the pieces fit together, apply construction adhesive to the inside of the connector fittings and insert the ends of the copper pipe to form the canopy frame. Let dry.

- Step 9: Apply construction adhesive to the inside of the the bottom of the "T" fittings and insert the canopy posts. Let dry.

- Step 10: Slide the canopy posts down over the threaded metal rods.

- Step 11: Measure the muslin to make the bed curtains, allowing the fabric to "puddle" on the floor to hide the risers at the bottom of the bed.

- Step 12: Wash and dry the muslin, allowing it to crinkle. Do not press or hem.

- Step 13: If desired, sew additional fabric to the top of the muslin. Set aside.

- Step 14: Sand the entire bed and canopy and wipe clean.

- Step 15: Using a damp sponge, sponge over the entire bed and canopy with black paint. Let dry.

- Step 16: Repeat Step 15 with metallic copper paint.

- Step 17: Repeat Step 15 with brown paint.

- Step 18: Using a foam brush, seal the entire bed and canopy. Let dry.

- Step 19: Attach the bed curtains to the drapery clips.

MOSAIC MIRROR

This is a $5 mirror from the thrift store. I added precut mirrored tiles that I had purchased in circle and square shapes from the local craft store.

I started on the outer rim of the mirror, working inward to create a mosaic pattern. The mirrored tiles are attached with clear mirror glue—you can really get creative with this one. There is no end to the possibilities here!

Second-hand mirrors are readily available at most thrift stores and come in all shapes and sizes. Another good source for acquiring old mirrors is yard sales. Don't worry if the mirror is chipped on the edges, the mirrored tiles will be covering the damaged areas!

PRESSED FLOWER PICTURE

These pressed flower pictures are a direct result of the perennial flowerbeds that grace our front yard. I save all of my old phone books and use them as flower presses. The frames used for these one-of-a-kind pieces are collected from second-hand shops and yard sales. Most of the frames were purchased without glass, but for a few dollars, you can have glass custom-cut to size.

An old French book found at the thrift store was used as backing for the flowers. The book was preserved by having the pages photocopied and then distressing the copies to look aged.

MATERIALS

- Frame with glass
- Photocopied pages from an old book
- Synthetic sponge
- Craft paint: gold
- Iron
- Pressed flowers
- Cellophane tape
- White chalk
- Aerosol hairspray
- Heavy-weight cardboard
- Brown packing paper
- Masking tape
- Rubber cement

WHAT TO DO

• Step 1: Crinkle the photocopied pages. Wet the pages, then squeeze out the excess water.

• Step 2: Open the wet pages and lay them as flat as possible.

• Step 3: Using a damp sponge, lightly rub the crinkled pages with gold paint, allowing some paint to settle in the crevices.
Let dry until damp.

• Step 4: Using an iron on low heat, press the damp pages until they are flat and dry.

• Step 5: Arrange the pressed flowers on the painted pages as desired.

• Step 6: Secure the pressed flowers to the painted pages with rubber cement.

• Step 7: Place a strip of cellophane tape over each flower, overlapping the tape onto the painted page.

• Step 8: Go over the cellophane tape on the edge overlapped to the page with white chalk. Rub around the edge of the cellophane tape so it is outlined with chalk, then smear the chalk on the edges of the tape.

• Step 9: Spray the pages with aerosol hairspray to set.

• Step 10: Measure and cut a piece of heavy-weight cardboard to fit inside the frame.

• Step 11: Cut the brown packing paper to fit over the piece of cardboard, allowing a 3" overhang on each side.

• Step 12: Crinkle the brown packing paper. Wet the paper, then squeeze out the excess water.

• Step 13: Open the wet paper and lay it as flat as possible. Let dry until damp.

• Step 14: Using an iron on low heat, press the damp paper until it is flat and dry.

• Step 15: Tape the packing paper to the piece of cardboard with masking tape. The 3" over-hang should be pulled to the back of the card-board.

• Step 16: Adhere the pressed flower pages onto the packing paper with rubber cement.

• Step 17: Mount the completed pressed flower picture inside the frame.

• Step 18: Adhere packing paper to the back side of the frame with rubber cement. Let dry.

FERN TOPIARIES

I love topiaries! They add such great height for tablescaping. You can use a topiary anywhere you would normally put a houseplant. Take into consideration that they don't need watering, feeding, or pruning!

MATERIALS

- Drill & $^1/_{16}$" bit

- Stick: desired height

- Branches of dried fern

- Dry post mix: 1 bag

- Vase or planter

- Hot-glue gun & glue sticks

- Dried moss or small pebbles

- Spray bottle

- Insecticide soap

WHAT TO DO

- Step 1: Drill holes into, but not through, the stick, near the top, to support the branches of dried fern.

If you are making a multilevel topiary, drill a series of holes into the stick in selected sections.

- Step 2: Mix the dry post mix with water until it is the consistency of dough. Place it in the bottom of the vase or planter until it is at least 1/3 full. Allow the post mix to partially set.

Overfilling the vase or planter with post mix may cause the container to crack.

- Step 3: Place the bottom end of the stick into the partially set post mix. Center and straighten the stick and let dry.

- Step 4: Using scissors, carefully clip the branches of dried fern into small manageable sections. These sections should resemble live foliage.

- Step 5: Working from the bottom up, dip the end of each dried fern "branch" into hot glue and quickly push into one of the predrilled holes.

- Step 6: Fill the vase or planter with dried moss or small pebbles to cover the post mix.

- Step 7: Spray the topiary and vase or planter with insecticide soap. Let dry.

Spraying will prevent house mites from making a home in your new creation. Spray the topiary on the average of once a month to prevent future infestations.

FENCE POST SCULPTURES

These delightful sculptures will add instant charm to any room in your home. They can be painted and weathered to match any decor or they can stand on their own.

Taking such little time and money to create, they are sure to yield much in return. The idea for these was born after we had built the fence surrounding our home. We had an ample supply of scraps to use, store, or discard. I put most of the scraps to use as these fence post sculptures and gave them as Christmas gifts. The only parts I had to buy were the wooden finials for the tops.

MATERIALS FOR THREE SCULPTURES

- Treated fence post:
  4" x 4" x 6'

- 3 Wooden finials

- Synthetic sponge

- Craft paints:
  to match your decor

- 100-grit sandpaper

- Hot-glue gun & glue sticks

- Dried moss

WHAT TO DO

- Step 1: Cut the fence post into desired lengths to create the sculpture bases.

- Step 2: Screw the wooden finials onto the top of each sculpture base.

- Step 3: Using a damp sponge, lightly streak paint over the sculptures. Let dry.

- Step 4: Lightly sand off some of the paint, allowing portions of the wood to show through.

- Step 5: Hot-glue the strands of dried moss onto the sculptures to simulate a vine.

DECORATING TIPS

- Pair these sculptures with other garden elements such as a bird's nest or dried flowers.

- Use fence post sculptures as easels for small framed botanicals.

BROWN PACKING PAPER WALLPAPER

This project originated from the necessity to cover partially removed wallpaper. Because the room was paneled underneath, glue had been used to secure some of the wallpaper, making it almost impossible to ever totally remove all of it.

I wanted a quick and inexpensive solution. The idea for brown packing paper wallpaper was born!

This technique is so simple, I actually paid my 10-year-old son to "paper" all the centers of the walls. I finished the edges and corners.

MATERIALS

- Brown packing paper
- Nylon paintbrush: 6" flat
- Heavy-duty, water-soluble wallpaper paste: 1 gallon
- Smoothing spatula
- Craft knife
- Craft paint: taupe
- Synthetic sponge

WHAT TO DO

- Step 1: Tear sections of the packing paper into various shapes and sizes.

- Step 2: Using a paintbrush, apply the wallpaper paste to the wall, working in about 5' sections.

- Step 3: One piece at a time, crinkle the packing paper. Wet the paper, then squeeze out the excess water.

- Step 4: Open the wet pieces of paper and smooth them onto the wall with a smoothing spatula.

- Step 5: Using the paintbrush, go over the pieces of packing paper you just applied with more wallpaper paste. Make certain the outer edges are flush with the wall.

If creases occur in the center of the piece of paper, leave them. It will add to the effect when it dries and the wet paper is vulnerable to tearing if you try to remove the crease.

123

• Step 6: Continue adding the wet pieces of paper until all the centers of the walls are covered.

• Step 7: To paper the edges and corners, use the flat edge of the packing paper, tearing only one side. Use the flat edge to cover the top, bottom, and sides of the walls. Trim away any excess with a sharp craft knife. Let dry.

• Step 8: Mix equal parts of taupe paint and wallpaper paste to create a glazing medium and sealer.

• Step 9: Using a damp sponge, lightly apply the taupe glaze/sealer over the walls. Let dry. When it dries, the "color" will rest in all of the creases and around all of the overlapping seams.

• Step 10: Using the sponge, apply a light coat of wallpaper paste over the wallpaper. This gives it a durable surface for cleaning and a soft sheen.

The color possibilities for this technique are limitless. This is a terra-cotta wash instead of the taupe used in the master bath. It has a warmer feel and its intensity can be increased through additional color washes.

For a more dramatic effect resembling leather, try sponging the color wash on as shown in the photo above instead of using the washing method.

GOLD-LEAFED TOWEL SHELF

What an ugly duckling this bookcase-turned-towel-shelf used to be. It was a bright shade of gold and heavily damaged when I picked it up at the thrift store for $6.

It sat in our garage for over a year, surviving three separate sessions of heavy-duty cleaning. I finally decided to give it some thought and this gold-leafed towel shelf was soon hanging above the toilet in the master bath.

MATERIALS

- Bookcase
- 100-grit sandpaper
- Nylon paintbrush: 6" flat
- Flat latex paint: black, brown
- Gold leafing
- Foam brush: 2" flat
- Satin acrylic sealer
- Wood screws

WHAT TO DO

- Step 1: Lightly sand the bookcase and wipe clean.

- Step 2: Using a paintbrush, apply a base coat of black paint onto the bookcase. Let dry.

- Step 3: Using the paintbrush, lightly streak brown paint over the coat of black to simulate wood grain. Let dry.

- Step 4: Apply gold leafing over all of the edges of the bookcase to accentuate any outstanding features.

- Step 5: Using a foam brush, seal the bookcase. Let dry.

- Step 6: Additional coats of sealer may be applied. Let dry between each coat.

- Step 7: Decide where you are going to hang the "towel shelf." If studs are available in the wall, use wood screws to hang the bookcase.

If studs are not available, use molly bolts to hang the bookcase. When using molly bolts, predrill pilot holes in the bookcase and in the wall.

- Step 8: Hoist the bookcase into mounting position and secure it onto the wall.

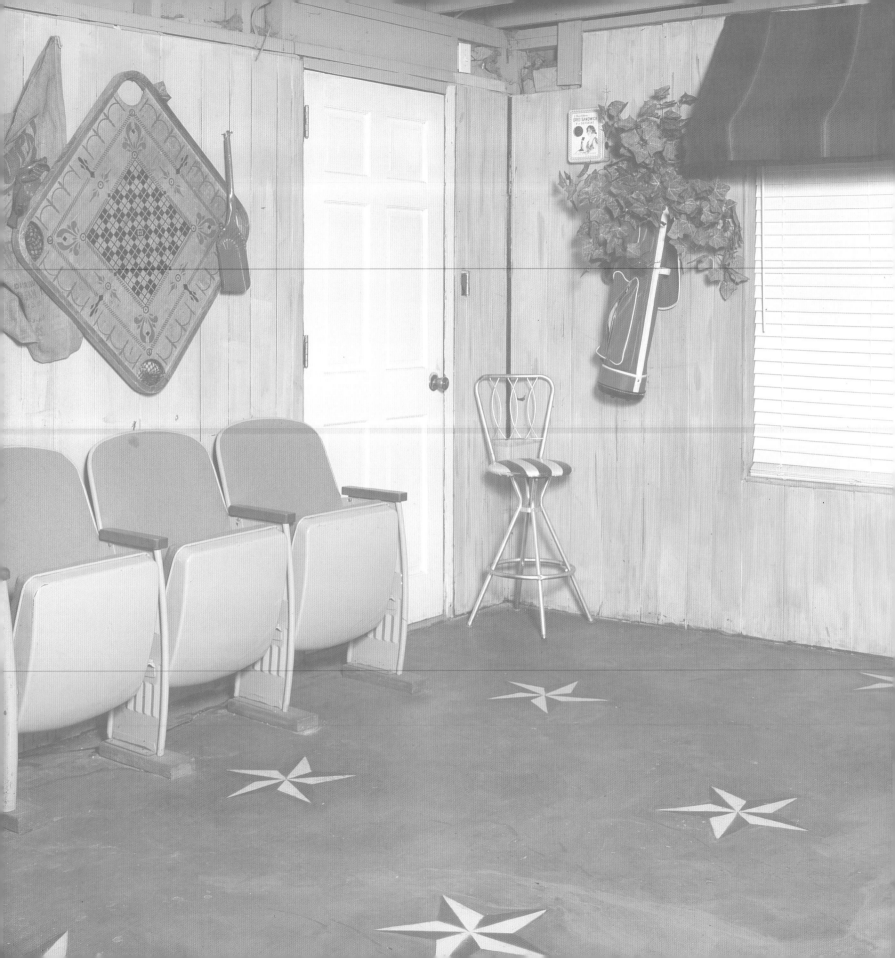

THE REST
OF THE HOUSE

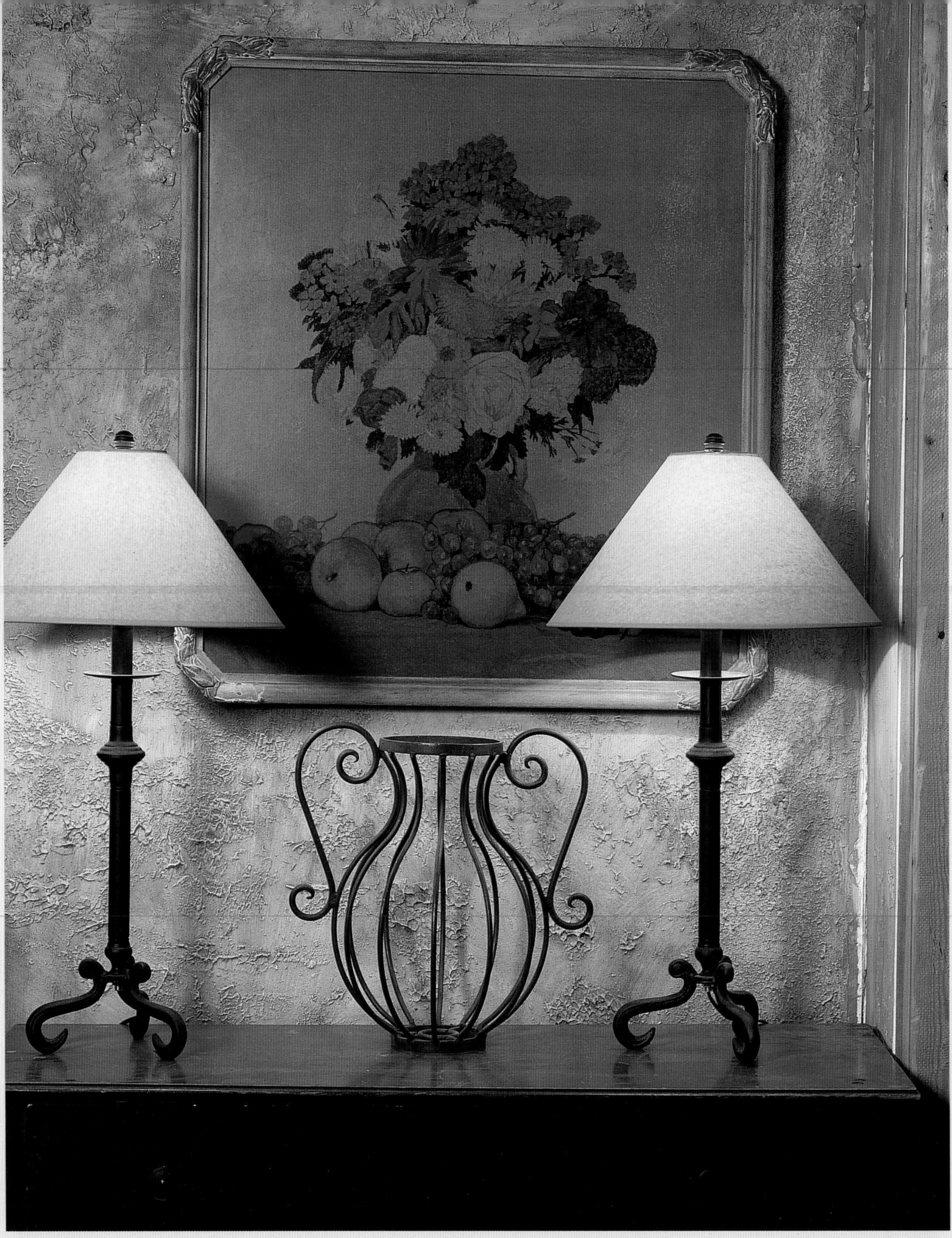

TUSCANY-STYLE STUCCO

One box of wallboard joint compound can go a long way in the decorating scheme of things. That is the magic used here to create this European country wall texture. Together, with a synthetic sponge and two colors of craft paint, you can transform a sterile room into a cozy hideaway.

At night when we come to this room to watch a movie or play games, it feels like the warm glow of a fireplace.

The rich terra-cotta makes everything placed against it stand out.

MATERIALS

- Putty knife

- Wallboard joint compound: 1 box

- Synthetic sponge

- Craft paints: gold, terra-cotta

WHAT TO DO

• Step 1: Start with a white or off-white wall and work in about 5' sections. Using a putty knife, apply joint compound to the walls.

• Step 2: Partially smooth out the joint compound, then push against it with the flat side of the putty knife to create the desired amount of texture.

STEP 1

• Step 3: Blend the next sections as you continue until the entire wall(s) is textured. Small sections of bare wall should appear between the texture to add variation. Let dry.

• Step 4: Mix one part terra-cotta paint to one part water. Using a damp sponge, lightly apply the terra-cotta wash over the textured wall(s). Let dry.

• Step 5: Mix one part gold paint to one part water. Using a damp sponge, lightly apply the gold wash over the textured wall(s). Let dry.

Additional coats of wash may be added until the desired color intensity is achieved.

STEP 2

STEP 4

FRENCH PROVINCIAL CHEST

This is yet another thrift-store find. It is actually a piece of French provincial bedroom furniture. Furniture like this is frequently available through the classified ads or found at yard sales. The top is laminate and the front is a plastic wood veneer. With just the right touches, it looks like a million!

MATERIALS

- French provincial chest
- 200-grit sandpaper
- Synthetic sponge
- Craft paints: brown, metallic gold, salmon, verdigris
- Wallpaper: green marble
- Foam brush: 2" flat
- Satin acrylic sealer

WHAT TO DO

- Step 1: Sand the chest and wipe clean.

- Step 2: Using a damp sponge, randomly sponge salmon paint onto the front of the chest, allowing some of the white and gold from the existing veneer to show through. Let dry.

- Step 3: Using the sponge, randomly sponge brown paint onto the edges of the drawers and the corners of the chest. Let dry.

- Step 4: Using the sponge, randomly sponge verdigris paint onto the design on the drawers, allowing some of the gold from the existing design to show through. Let dry.

- Step 5: Position the wallpaper over the top of the chest and outline the top. Cut the wallpaper into the traced shape and adhere to the top of the chest. Let dry.

- Step 6: Using a foam brush, randomly apply metallic gold paint to the edges of the drawers and around the top lip of the chest. Let dry.

- Step 7: Using the foam brush, seal the chest. Let dry.

DECORATING TIPS

- Use this technique on any furniture piece with raised decorative panels.

- Try gold or silver leafing on a chest such as this.

CHALK-BOARD WALL

You will be the most popular mom on the block! Kids of all ages love to write on the wall, so why not give them an entire room of walls to doodle on!

The magic of this project lies in a gallon of black flat latex paint. Simply paint over the existing wall and let dry. Apply a second coat for cleaning durability. It washes up beautifully with a damp sponge.

All you need to add . . . kids and chalk!

DECORATING TIPS

• Green flat latex paint can be used instead of black.

• Paint the back side of a flat door and turn it into a giant memo door— great for teenagers!

PANELED WALL MAKEOVER

Underneath the sunny glow of these game room walls lies dark and depressing paneling. This is supposed to be a happy room to do fun things in. The walls had to undergo a dramatic makeover—without major expense.

The walls were cleaned, sanded, painted in layers, and sanded again to achieve a seemingly indestructible surface to house teenage party animals. Now when they are "goin' at it" the walls need not be a concern. Any added weathering will just add to the overall look of the room!

MATERIALS

- Industrial-strength cleaner
- 100-grit sandpaper
- Nylon paintbrush: 6" flat
- Semigloss paints: cream, sunset orange, sunshine yellow
- Synthetic sponge

WHAT TO DO

• Step 1: Clean the walls with an industrial-strength cleaner.

• Step 2: Sand the paneling and wipe clean.

• Step 3: Using a paintbrush, apply a base coat of sunset orange paint in a streaking motion, moving vertically over the paneling, allowing portions of the paneling to show through. Let dry.

• Step 4: Repeat Step 3 with sunshine yellow paint, allowing portions of the sunset orange paint and the paneling to show through. Let dry.

• Step 5: Repeat Step 3 with cream paint, allowing portions of the previous layers of paint and the paneling to show through. Do not let paint dry completely.

• Step 6: Using a damp sponge, gently rub over the cream layer to blend into the previous layers of paint. Let dry.

• Step 7: Sand the painted paneling in selected areas to simulate the look of natural weathering.

STENCILED FLOOR

The trick here was to come up with a practical solution for flooring in the downstairs game room. Our teenagers frequently hosted parties here, so we needed to be able to clean up party messes easily. The optimal solution would be to install a drain in the middle of the floor to be able to hose the entire room down for cleaning. That obviously wasn't a practical solution, so we opted for an alternate. We would paint the floor and add stencils for fun and interest, seal it with an acrylic sealer, and call it good.

MATERIALS

- Industrial-strength cleaner
- Clean rags
- Flat latex paint: dove gray
- Straightedge
- Craft knife
- Poster board
- Masking tape
- High-gloss spray paints: red, yellow
- Paint roller with an extension handle & pan
- Satin acrylic sealer

WHAT TO DO

- Step 1: Thoroughly clean the floor with an industrial-strength cleaner. Let dry.

- Step 2: Using clean rags, rub a base coat of dove gray latex paint onto sections of the concrete floor, allowing portions of the concrete to show through. This gives a built-in layer of color. In addition, the latex paint will partially soak into the floor acting as a self-sealer to the concrete. Let dry.

- Step 3: Using a straight-edge and a sharp craft knife, cut a star stencil from the poster board. You will only need to cut one side of the star; you will be flipping it over to do the opposite side.

- Step 4: Measure the floor surface and determine the placement of the stars. Place the stencil on the floor and secure the edges with masking tape.

- Step 5: Paint the stencil in selected locations with high-gloss red spray paint. Let dry.

- Step 6: Flip the stencil over. Paint the stencil in selected locations with high-gloss yellow spray paint. Let dry.

- Step 7: Using a paint roller with an extension handle, seal the entire floor surface. Let dry.

GUEST BATH CABINET

This cabinet had been custom-sized to fit into this smaller bathroom space. The budget did not allow us to replace it. An old sink was replaced and molding added over the counter top.

I painted scenery in oil paints over the existing cabinet using the same method as the Scenery-Painted Lockers on page 147. New hardware was installed.

These inexpensive changes transformed this tiny, uninspired bathroom into a welcome reprieve with a view! The oil-based paint allows for an easy clean-up with soap and water.

FAUX STONE FLOOR

If you have always loved the look of stone floors, but never have it in the budget, this could be a solution for you! The floor is concrete that has not been sealed. The paint is a series of three different layers that are applied in stages. If there are "real" cracks in the floor, it will only add to the authenticity of the stone appearance. The faux onyx diamonds are black adhesive-backed paper applied to the floor and sealed.

MATERIALS

- Industrial-strength cleaner
- Clean rags
- Flat latex paints: cream, gold, taupe
- Plastic grocery bags
- Craft knife
- Adhesive-backed paper
- Paint roller with an extension handle & pan
- Satin acrylic sealer

WHAT TO DO

- Step 1: Thoroughly clean the floor with an industrial-strength cleaner. Let dry.

- Step 2: Using clean rags, rub a base coat of taupe paint onto sections of the concrete floor, allowing portions of the concrete to show through. This gives a built-in layer of color. In addition, the latex paint will partially soak into the floor acting as a self-sealer to the concrete. Let dry.

- Step 3: Crinkle a plastic grocery bag and dip it into gold paint. Wipe off excess paint to avoid dripping.

- Step 4: Randomly "rag" the floor over the coat of taupe. Let dry.

- Step 5: Repeat Steps 3–4 with cream paint, allowing portions of all previous layers of paint to show through.

- Step 6: Measure the floor surface and determine the placement of the diamonds. Using a sharp craft knife, cut the diamonds in the desired size from the adhesive-backed paper and apply.

- Step 7: Using a paint roller with an extension handle, seal the entire floor surface. Let dry.

SCENERY-PAINTED LOCKERS

This formerly plain white storage space which had been recycled from the kitchen remodeling was in desperate need of some help. My laundry room was void of windows so the space felt claustrophobic. By "removing" the storage wall and painting a seashore vista in its place, the laundry room became a favorite place for the kids to play and for mom to do the laundry!

MATERIALS

- Nylon paintbrush: 6" flat
- Satin latex paint: white
- Craft paints: amber, powder blue, sky blue, gray, dark green, leaf green, taupe, white
- High-gloss acrylic polyurethane sealer

WHAT TO DO

- Step 1: Using a paintbrush, apply a base coat of white latex paint onto the storage lockers.

- Step 2: Next to the top edge, brush a small amount of sky blue craft paint onto the lockers. Blend the bottom edge into the coat of white. Do not let paint dry completely.

- Step 3: Dry-brush powder blue craft paint into the bottom edge of the coat of sky blue. Continue from top to bottom two-thirds of the way down the lockers. Do not let paint dry completely.

- Step 4: Randomly paint sections with white craft paint to create the bases for the clouds. Let dry.

- Step 5: Using the edge of the paintbrush and a pouncing motion, feather in the clouds with white craft paint over the top of the cloud bases. Blend with a horizontal stroke. Let dry.

- Step 6: Feather a small amount of amber craft paint along the bottom edges of the clouds to simulate sunlight. Let dry.

- Step 7: Feather in the shoreline with amber craft paint. Blend the bottom edge into the coat of white. Do not let paint dry completely.

• Step 8: Feather in the foliage with dark green and leaf green craft paints. Let dry.

• Step 9: Working in horizontal strokes, paint the water with powder blue craft paint, allowing portions of the base coat color to show through. Let dry.

• Step 10: Using the edge of the paintbrush, cut in the waves with gray craft paint. Blend the waves into the bottom edge of the shoreline. Working in horizontal strokes, dry-brush the waves to blend into the water. Let dry.

• Step 11: Using the paintbrush, seal the lockers. Let dry.

• Step 12: Additional coats of sealer may be applied. Let dry between each coat.

COBBLESTONE

This is another project you can recruit your kids to help you with. My 13-year-old daughter and her friend helped stamp the basic bricks onto the concrete floor that had previously been painted white. I did the shading and detail work. It transformed a dreary space into an enchanted "courtyard" right inside my laundry room. By adding the painted moss growth between the bricks, it makes this space feel like it's alive!

MATERIALS

- Nylon paintbrush: 6" flat

- Synthetic sponge shaped like a brick

- Craft paints: gray, dark green, leaf green, brick-red, white, yellow

- Fan-shaped paintbrush

- Paint roller with an extension handle & pan

- Satin acrylic sealer

WHAT TO DO

- Step 1: Using a 6" flat paintbrush, load the brick-shaped sponge with brick-red, gray, and white paints.

- Step 2: Lightly press the sponge onto the floor, creating a pattern of staggered rows. Leave approximately 1" between each brick and each row. Continue until the sponge needs to be reloaded, then continue until the floor is covered with "bricks." Let dry for 24 hours or more.

- Step 3: Dilute gray craft paint with a small amount of water. Using a damp sponge, lightly apply the gray wash over the entire floor, wiping off some of the gray that rests on the bricks. Let dry.

- Step 4: Using a fan-shaped paintbrush and a pouncing motion, go over a small section of grout with dark green, leaf green, and yellow paints, slightly overlapping the surrounding brick. Let dry.

- Step 5: Randomly shade around the bricks with a pencil to imitate different heights.

- Step 6: Using a paint roller with an extension handle, seal the entire floor surface. Let dry.

- Step 7: Additional coats of sealer may be applied. Let dry between each coat.

FAUX RAISED COPPER PANELS

These metal doors, purchased for $5 per pair from the thrift store, were used as panels for our daughter's wedding, but they would be fabulous as functional doors.

The "relief" is embossed wallpaper border and ceiling medallions cut in half. The edges were caulked to secure and hide any seams. The metal nature of the doors adds to the illusion of them actually being made of copper. When you touch the doors, you cannot tell that they are not.

MATERIALS

- Metal louvered doors

- 100-grit sandpaper

- Embossed wallpaper border

- Ceiling medallions

- Paintable acrylic latex caulk

- Spray paint: flat black, metallic copper

- Synthetic sponge

- Craft paints: metallic copper, verdigris

WHAT TO DO

- Step 1: Sand the metal doors and wipe clean.

- Step 2: Measure, cut, and install the wallpaper border and ceiling medallions in the desired area(s). Let dry.

- Step 3: Caulk all the edges and seams. Let dry.

- Step 4: Paint the metal doors with flat black spray paint. Let dry.

- Step 5: Randomly spray over the coat of flat black with metallic copper spray paint. Let dry.

- Step 6: Using a damp sponge, randomly sponge verdigris craft paint over the coats of flat black and metallic copper. Let dry.

- Step 7: Using the damp sponge, randomly sponge metallic copper craft paint onto the embossed areas of the wallpaper border, the raised areas of the ceiling medallions, and along the edges of the louvers. Let dry.

OUT & ABOUT

PAINTED EXTERIOR BRICK

The outside of the house was plain, dirty, white brick when we moved in. We had learned from a professional painter that exterior brick can be painted using exterior latex paint. The paint soaks into the brick creating a durable surface for cleaning.

I painted the brick trim over all the exterior doors and windows using the same technique as I had used on the Fireplace Bricks on page 54. For the remaining brick, I rented a paint spray gun and sprayed the brick with a battleship gray exterior latex paint. The paint looks as good as the day I first did it nearly nine years later!

FLOWER BED

If you have a sunny spot in your garden and a brass bed that has no home, why not transform it into a brass "flower bed" and add some whimsy to your landscape? This bed was simply positioned to catch the eye as well as the sun, allowing the plants, flowers, and herbs to flourish within.

Thrift stores and yard sales are often stocked with an old brass day bed or two for a similar effect. If the bed is tarnished and worn—all the better. It will have a head start on the natural weathering it will receive in your garden.

DECORATING TIPS

• Sweet peas and other small vining flowers would accentuate the vertical lines of the bed and give your landscape some vertical interest.

• Stand or mount a brass headboard next to your back door to use as a rack for hanging flowers or herbs to dry.

FAUX-FINISHED GARDEN URN

This urn looked great to begin with so I didn't have to do too much to it.

The base coat was a warm gold with just a touch of black. I wanted it to look a little more aged so I sponged black craft paint onto it until it seemed adequate to me. Because the urn already had a rough texture, it allowed the new layer of paint to remain on the top for a two-dimensional effect. This really accentuated the raised elements and brought them to center stage.

The urn was sealed with an acrylic sealer so it could be placed in my garden.

METRIC CONVERSIONS

INCHES TO MILLIMETRES AND CENTIMETRES

MM-Millimetres   CM-Centimetres

INCHES	MM	CM	INCHES	CM	INCHES	CM
$1/8$	3	0.9	9	22.9	30	76.2
$1/4$	6	0.6	10	25.4	31	78.7
$3/8$	10	1.0	11	27.9	32	81.3
$1/2$	13	1.3	12	30.5	33	83.8
$5/8$	16	1.6	13	33.0	34	86.4
$3/4$	19	1.9	14	35.6	35	88.9
$7/8$	22	2.2	15	38.1	36	91.4
1	25	2.5	16	40.6	37	94.0
$1\,1/4$	32	3.2	17	43.2	38	96.5
$1\,1/2$	38	3.8	18	45.7	39	99.1
$1\,3/4$	44	4.4	19	48.3	40	101.6
2	51	5.1	20	50.8	41	104.1
$2\,1/2$	64	6.4	21	53.3	42	106.7
3	76	7.6	22	55.9	43	109.2
$3\,1/2$	89	8.9	23	58.4	44	111.8
4	102	10.2	24	61.0	45	114.3
$4\,1/2$	114	11.4	25	63.5	46	116.8
5	127	12.7	26	66.0	47	119.4
6	152	15.2	27	68.6	48	121.9
7	178	17.8	28	71.1	49	124.5
8	203	20.3	29	73.7	50	127.0

YARDS TO METRES

YARDS	METRES	YARDS	METRES	YARDS	METRES	YARDS	METRES	YARDS	METRES
$1/8$	0.11	$2\,1/8$	1.94	$4\,1/8$	3.77	$6\,1/8$	5.60	$8\,1/8$	7.43
$1/4$	0.23	$2\,1/4$	2.06	$4\,1/4$	3.89	$6\,1/4$	5.72	$8\,1/4$	7.54
$3/8$	0.34	$2\,3/8$	2.17	$4\,3/8$	4.00	$6\,3/8$	5.83	$8\,3/8$	7.66
$1/2$	0.46	$2\,1/2$	2.29	$4\,1/2$	4.11	$6\,1/2$	5.94	$8\,1/2$	7.77
$5/8$	0.57	$2\,5/8$	2.40	$4\,5/8$	4.23	$6\,5/8$	6.06	$8\,5/8$	7.89
$3/4$	0.69	$2\,3/4$	2.51	$4\,3/4$	4.34	$6\,3/4$	6.17	$8\,3/4$	8.00
$7/8$	0.80	$2\,7/8$	2.63	$4\,7/8$	4.46	$6\,7/8$	6.29	$8\,7/8$	8.12
1	0.91	3	2.74	5	4.57	7	6.40	9	8.23
$1\,1/8$	1.03	$3\,1/8$	2.86	$5\,1/8$	4.69	$7\,1/8$	6.52	$9\,1/8$	8.34
$1\,1/4$	1.14	$3\,1/4$	2.97	$5\,1/4$	4.80	$7\,1/4$	6.63	$9\,1/4$	8.46
$1\,3/8$	1.26	$3\,3/8$	3.09	$5\,3/8$	4.91	$7\,3/8$	6.74	$9\,3/8$	8.57
$1\,1/2$	1.37	$3\,1/2$	3.20	$5\,1/2$	5.03	$7\,1/2$	6.86	$9\,1/2$	8.69
$1\,5/8$	1.49	$3\,5/8$	3.31	$5\,5/8$	5.14	$7\,5/8$	6.97	$9\,5/8$	8.80
$1\,3/4$	1.60	$3\,3/4$	3.43	$5\,3/4$	5.26	$7\,3/4$	7.09	$9\,3/4$	8.92
$1\,7/8$	1.71	$3\,7/8$	3.54	$5\,7/8$	5.37	$7\,7/8$	7.20	$9\,7/8$	9.03
2	1.83	4	3.66	6	5.49	8	7.32	10	9.14

INDEX